Rio Grande Ripples

By

Mabel Steele Wright

Steele Park Press

To the Memory of my Mountain Man

RAY WRIGHT

"If Winter comes . . ."

Top: Big Ridge, Clear Creek County
Center: The Ranch snowed under
Bottom: Taking off weight (ranch-shed roof)

" . . . can Spring be far behind?
Top: The Rio Grande in flood stage
Center: The Ranch smiling through
Bottom: Workman Ranch, Creede, Colorado

Top: "The cattle are standing like statues"
Center: Big Ridge stands guard on the meadow
Bottom: Feed racks for calves in winter

Emmett Workman

Ray Wright
My Mountain Man

Rio Grande Ripples

Prologue

These things I love: currant bushes in the sun, columbines in the rain, little brown-eyed boys, and this ranch on the Rio Grande.

If I live to be a hundred-five, which I may well do - it would be just like me! - feeble, halt and blind, as long as the one faculty, Memory, remains to me, picturing the people, the places, the many incidents of the past, I shall never lack for entertainment.

Surely, anyone interested enough to read the pages of this little book will readily understand how much more could have been written. In fact, it was difficult to make a stopping place. But I do not want these vignettes to be boring; and above all, I wish to stress that nothing in these pages is intended to hurt anyone.

To any readers of this little book, I want to say that is was not my intention to make it a treatise on myself. It has been said that almost anybody's life would make a story and I believe this. Also, I have not written for self aggrandizement. Rather, it has been a real labor of love to write about a few of the many who came into this area.

I have left out several for various reasons. I have not been able to obtain authentic history of some. Others have already received publicity of some sort. For others I have felt a sense of inadequacy in trying to do them justice. Among the latter is the Soward family that begins with the arrival of

Jackson Soward about 1873. The history of this family down to the fifth generation would make a fair-sized book itself. Scarcely a contract, deed or any other legal paper concerning land transactions, from Del Norte where the Sowards held property, on up miles above Creede along the Rio Grande, fails to show the Soward name. They were people with foresight and much business ability - "men (and women!) to match our mountains." I am most fortunate in being able to count Mrs. Emma Soward McCrone as a friend - I have none dearer and/or better.

[Ed. This book comprises both River Ripples and Rio Grande Recollections.]

There was Aunt Jennie, a product of her time no worse and no better than many of her sex. Report has it that she had come from God-knows-where to youthful, blooming, roistering Creede, where she danced in flesh-colored tights on the bars and tables of the saloons and otherwise entertained the patrons. Be this true or false - and nobody remembers - Jennie ("Aunt" was added as she accumulated years) married a good-natured fellow, known as Uncle Charlie, and went to live on his ranch some fifteen miles or so up the river. She assisted her husband in stock raising. One account says that a friend accompanied her on this initial visit; but after looking the situation over - it is beautiful country - Jennie proceeded to "run" the other woman off, assumed command of her domain, and in due time became what we call a "character." She was not unique, as there were several characters in those good old days; but some of the incidents in which she was concerned are worth recording.

Aunt Jennie had a lot of troubles, large and small. One day with the gentlest of breezes and a blue sky dotted with just enough cloud pillows, "perfect fishing weather," she went down to the Rio Grande to catch a mess of trout. She was clad, as she often was, in a pair of Uncle Charlie's bib-over- alls. He always bought clothes a size too large, and he was a big man; so the overalls fit Aunt Jennie, who was of moderate dimensions, adequately and then some.

By this time the ridge road had been practically abandoned, and travel was by the river. Aunt Jennie fished, moving along the river's bank and enjoying the fine day. Meanwhile, the breeze had strengthened somewhat, and in making a cast as she stepped through the grasses and wild geraniums (bending over slightly), the wind carried her line backward and the hook caught in the ample seat of her overalls. Now, if you have ever had such an experience, you know how it is; and if you haven't, all I can say is, it's often a little difficult to remove a fishhook embarbed where one can't see it! Aunt Jennie was struggling valiantly, undecided whether to remove the overalls, when along the road came one Lee Barber with a neighbor in a buckboard.

"Lee," called Aunt J., "come here and see if you can get this dadgummed fishhook outta my pants!"

"Sure," answered Lee, jumped down, and went to the rescue of the lady in distress.

After considerable finagling, and what appeared to be sincere efforts to extract the hook, he told Aunt J. he believed he'd have to cut it out. She enjoined him to go ahead. Out came his pocket knife and the largest blade. Then, gathering up all the slack in the pants, he proceeded to cut out the hook, leaving an immense hole . . . and so much of Aunt Jennie exposed as might resemble a full moon newly risen!

Lee ran to his wagon, and he and his companion were off down the road, followed by Aunt Jennie's vociferous and colorful remarks and a few rocks fairly expertly though futilely thrown.

In the beginning, the main highway did not follow its present route up the river, and a few miles below Uncle Charlie's and Aunt Jennie's ranch it climbed over what is called the "Big Ridge." However, cattlemen of the San Luis Valley who grazed their herds in the mountain area on the upper Rio Grande, especially if the herd was small, liked to follow the river road. It was easier on man and beast. There were water and good grass in the mountain meadows along the way and fewer rocks. Aunt Jennie's special job in the spring and fall was to maintain a watch over that part of the ranch along which the river and road ran chummily; and she endeavored to keep "outside" stock from eating up the grass to which she felt her own cattle were entitled, while her fenced meadows grew "hay."

Once little Johnny McClure, of Del Norte, was moving his cattle in for the summer, and he decided, upon reaching the forks of the road, to follow the river past Uncle Charlie's. Johnny's friend, Jim Workman, who lived a little farther up, was a bit of a character himself, and for various reasons he was not a friend of Aunt Jennie's. Knowing that she would be on hand to "whoop and holler" and otherwise "spook" Johnny's cows, he jumped on his cow pony and was off to the rescue. Sure enough, there were the cattle just rounding the turn and Aunt Jennie afoot - afoot being the first requisite for stampeding cattle - just opening her mouth for a lusty yell.

Then Jim came 'loping down suddenly upon her, brandishing several feet of good whip rope. There was just one thing to do, and Aunt Jennie did it. She took to the nearest, tallest and thickest clump of willows, and there she stayed while little Johnny McClure's cows wound their way past and on up the valley, with Johnny and Jim Workman riding "drag" and visiting.

Mr. Workman told me this tale, ending with his very special and personal expression - "the miserable bitch". I wish there were some way I could describe the sound of these words as he used them, but there is none. He used the expression to describe his feelings, and from the tone you knew just how he felt. I remember him saying the words while petting a small kitten which had strayed to his feet, and they were full of tenderness.

This upper Rio Grande country has afforded summer range for herds of cattle and flocks of sheep for many years. Many of these used to be driven from the San Luis Valley, grazing along the way. Since I had a father who thoroughly disliked sheep - "feathers, guts and all," as he put it - and having married a cow man with the same sentiments, except that he did enjoy lamb roasted or broiled and always ordered it if it was on the menu when we "ate out," it naturally followed that the cattlemen or riders who "looked after" cattle for the various cow outfits were the men who came into my life those first summers. They are all a part of the scene that passes before me now. I remember Bob Knapp, Hi Miller, Bill and Ted Walker, Cliff McCullough, Frank Stallard, Emmett Dabney, Clarence (Pete) Larrick, Gordon McCraney ... I could go on and on. Each seems to have a special niche in my memory.

The Walker brothers were English, unmistakable accents, especially Bill. The Mountain Man once stopped to visit with Tom Workman, who was repairing fence along the road in front of the Workman ranch, when a lone rider came along. Neither recognized him, though Tom said: "He's riding that old piebald of Shorty Fewell's - could be one of those English fellers." "Good morning, gentlemen!" said the rider, doffing his hat. " 'Ave you seen aught of a bloody bull? I am seeking one. The last I saw of 'im 'e was going over the 'orizon.'"

It was the English feller, of course. I recall certain colorful expressions of his, such as one describing a foolish person: "He acts like a goose that's been nicked on the 'ead"; or, " 'E's like a spring momin' - all soft and balmy." Good ol' Bill! He wandered far from the mountains he loved, to help build the "Big Inch" pipeline; and as he slept at the end of a day's labor, he passed quietly to a new and, for him, probably a better world.

Cliff McCullough, six feet four - even without his riding boots, though I never saw him in his socks - one of Pershing's own hand-picked guard in France during World War I, was a breaker of horses for Rube Fullington who had a place in the North Clear Creek country. I first saw Cliff as I came into the

Hermit Lakes post office, which was also the living room of the Masons. I stopped short and in horror. If there was a square inch of whole skin on his cheeks or on his aquiline nose, I could not see it.

"What happened?" I gasped.

"Oh, my horse and I had a little argument, and he piled me in a bunch of rocks and brush."

"But doesn't it hurt?"

"Na," and he smiled from his great height, the sweetest sort of a smile, such as you'd give a child who'd made a rather foolish albeit innocent remark. "A little hide don't matter. It'll grow again."

Cliff stayed with us two weeks in the late fall or early winter one year while he gathered some stray cattle for the Knapps, whose range was in that North Clear Creek area. Jimmie Workman was about three months old at the time, and when Tom was away Eleanor used to bring the baby and stay the night with us. When Cliff came in from his day's hard riding and found Eleanor here, he would quietly wash his face and hands, comb his wiry, darkish hair -he was certainly the strong, silent type - and then turn to Eleanor with: "Where's the kid?"

"On Mabel's bed. But he's awake - get him if you want to."

Away would go Cliff, carry Jimmie out to the living room and, folding up like a huge jackknife - how he managed it I could never figure out! - he'd seat himself on a little stool Ray had made for me. The stool wasn't over six inches high! There he would sit, holding Jimmie and murmuring funny little bits about the future the boy would have, the horses he'd ride, etc., until supper was ready.

Cliff was homely - but not the way we usually think it. It also means "unpretentious," and when I think of Cliff I see his face as he sat with that baby in his arms.

Each one of the three boys on the ranch had his own team of horses, and it was understood that none borrowed or used another's except under circumstances of dire necessity. Ray, at this particular time, had a bay and a black - Duke and Joe. They were gentle as the proverbial kittens, albeit with a few habits that discouraged alien hands from driving them. They would run away for much less reason than the drop of a hat, and they loved doing so. Ray never minded, it seemed, perhaps because this gave more assurance that they would not be borrowed often.

I recall one day when we were working on some fence among the willows at the lower ranch and had a wagon loaded with fence staves. I was holding a stave, while Ray nailed the wire onto it, when something touched off Duke and Joe - or maybe they just felt in the mood. Anyway, they were off scattering staves atop the tallest willows like candles thrown upon Christmas trees.

But there was one runaway incident that crowned them all. The Mountain Man took three fishermen to the Rio Grande above the Farmers' Union reservoir one summer day in 1917. He drove an outfit of a wagon known as "the hack" - one-, two- or three-seated, depending on the number of passengers. This day two seats were all that were required. Two of the men were schoolteachers, one from an Indian school in Oklahoma, and the other from Kansas. Both were past middle age, dignified gentlemen of the "schoolteacherish" type of stage and screen; neither would have said even so much as "dam!" They were pernickety to the nth degree, and grumpy besides. The third man, Bill Dolan, was just an ordinary sort of citizen to whom anything was agreeable.

Most systematically and seriously, they established a time for meeting that evening at one hour before sunset; and away with rods and creels they went.

Ray lazied most of the day, watched Bill fish awhile, looked for arrowheads in a bank of shale nearby, smoked, ate a sandwich, fed another to Duke and Joe along with their oats - they'd eat anything! - watered them, and thus the time wore away.

Soon Bill appeared with a creel full of fish, and they awaited the two "professors." The sun went down in the blaze of glory customary in these parts; the horses grew impatient and stamped their forefeet, turning to look back as if to inquire, "Why the delay?" But at Ray's, "Whoa, boys!" they did not stir.

At last the two belated fishermen came. They acknowledged the greetings of Ray and Bill rather testily, making it unnecessary to ask what luck they'd had fishing. With abruptness pleasing to Bill and Ray and the horses, they stowed their gear in the back, climbed in and seated themselves on the rear seat, leaving Bill to sit by Ray. Off for home they started, with Duke and Joe pulling steadily at a fast walk, their normal gait.

Silence reigned, except for the rattle of wheels and harness, but after a bit the two old gentlemen began a sort of terse, broken-up conversation with each other, ignoring Bill and Ray. One had a habit of running his words together: "Chilly-excessively-so-indeed." "Motorboat-just-starting-down-the-lake." "Were-we-in-that-rather-than-this-antiquated-equipage," and so forth.

Ray spoke up in his peculiar soft tone that presaged trouble. "Would you gentlemen like to reach the dam as soon as that boat?"

"Yes, young man, that is precisely what we would like."

With a quick aside to Bill, "Hold on! We are going for a ride!" Ray stood up, looped up a yard or so of the lines - he never carried a whip - walloped Joe across his fat posterior, and away they went! The hack was careening precariously, rocks flying from wheels and hooves. A side glance to the rear told Ray that the professors were holding on for dear life and limb. I don't think Ray exactly hoped one or both would fall out. On they raced, those happy horses, reaching the dam with the boat at least half a mile up the lake.   A slight rise in the roadbed made it easy to slow the horses to their walk - besides, they'd had their run and fun. Ray and Bill turned in accord to the two back-seat passengers. Both were gasping, and no two sheets were ever whiter. Gazing at each other, one said in a measured and sonorous tone: "Well, I had heard of these mountain drivers, but I never expected to ride with one of the SONSABITCHES!"

One lovely summer, while Ray and I were living on his homestead, we had a garden which included a strawberry bed. The latter was a rara avis, indeed, in this mountain country. This is not because strawberries do not do well, for a certain high-altitude variety known as "Everbearing" produce wonderfully, but the whole process involves labor, especially after the first year.

We were inordinately proud of ours, for though the bed was not extensive, we had all the berries we wanted. On occasion, we took some to the folks at headquarters. We had a milk cow that summer, too, another unusual situation on this cattle ranch, and we had strawberries and cream, and even strawberries and ice cream, just any ol' time.

One late afternoon we returned from a fence-building job across the river; and as we had gone right after breakfast, and had had no lunch, we naturally thought of strawberries and cream with good homemade bread 'n' butter. Out we went to pick a pint or two. I'm sure we did not notice any lack of big ripe berries; but we did note footprints of a small high-heeled lady's pumps here and there along the rows. We commented good-naturedly on what we'd do to "those smartie-dude gals if they don't stay outta our strawberries!"

The*Mountain Man said that, without our good cream, they'd have a bellyache "to who laid the chunk!"

This plunder occurred two or three other times that summer, so that always upon our return home we would hie ourselves to the strawberry bed to see if the heel prints were there.

Fall came, and what with hay harvest at the home ranch and all that involves, we forgot the strawberries and just about everything else. October arrived, and the gathering of cattle from the ranges began. Quite often some of the riders would stop in or Ray would bring them in with him.

One day Hi Miller ate lunch with us. When the strawberry preserves were passed, Hi asked if they had been made from our own berries. Before I could reply, he went on: "Those were the best berries I ever did eat! Did you know I stopped a couple of times, when you folks were away, and ate my dinner out in your garden?"

This hit the Mountain Man and me at one and the same instant. Hi was a small fellow, and his feet particularly so - right down dainty in a high-heeled cowboy boot! I doubt that he wore a boot over size four. So Hi was the "dude gal" who had walked in our strawberry bed! We explained, and all had a good laugh.

Well, he and the Mountain Man are doubtless reminiscing of this and other things beside some celestial stream now. . . .

Soon after my advent into the Wright regime, I noted that if the weather were inclement anywhere in the valley, winter or summer, spring or fall - and by "inclement" I mean it would be raining or snowing, according to the season - it would usually be storming up Trout Creek way.

One day I remarked to the Mountain Man, "I'll bet I know one person in this country who never curses the weather, and that's Brother Whozitt up Trout Creek, for he's been there so many years he must have resigned himself long ago."

"That's what you think!" replied the M.M., and then he explained. . . .

It seems this good dweller-up-the-creek - and a good man he was too, living as much the life of a Christian and a gentleman as he reasonably could - had the excellent habit of asking a blessing at each meal partaken at his board. One day the Mountain Man and a neighbor called on some ranch business - it was haying time, but rain had stopped that - and since it was the noon hour, they were, of course, invited to dine. As was his wont, Brother Bones thanked the good Lord for the food before them. The M.M. said it was a particularly beautifully worded prayer, and there was no doubt of his sincerity.

"Amen." Then: "Damn this damn wet weather to hell 'n' back! Didja ever see the like? Damn if I ever in these forty years! Damn it!"

So you see!

Weather! I could write a book! There are just two events in our lives up in these mountains that transpire regardless of the weather: birth and death; and in all my years here, the individuals concerned have all been considerate enough to time their great moments so as not to inconvenience their fellow men too greatly.

Of course, Marian Bent was born on a bitter day, and her father had to travel all those thirty-odd miles from Hermit Lakes to Creede on skis. But it really wasn't Marian's fault.

Her mother and father had gone soft, and her mother had moved to town for the event, rather than have her arrive at Hermit like sister Dorothy.

However the storm that was really a storm - "to who laid the chunk!" as the Mountain Man puts it - occurred in November, 1920. There were clouds this day before Thanksgiving - those feathery streamers that often presage snow. The fall had been a succession of beautiful, sunny days, with almost no moisture since hay harvest. As I drove away from the schoolhouse at Officer's ranch, I noted that the sky had become entirely overcast. The thought came to me that soon I might use my little sleigh. By the time I had sung "Sleep, Kentucky Babe" and hummed the "Black Hawk Waltz" four times, a few flakes of snow hit me on the nose. When I reached our ranch gate, my Mountain Man met me as usual to take care of my horse and we exchanged remarks, such as, "It's trying to snow." At supper time, only desultory flakes had fallen and the brown earth was still brown.

As we sat at the table, the telephone rang. It was Clayt Wetherill calling from the Sylvester place about five miles down the valley. He and "Red" Faunce had gone to Creede that afternoon in the Model-T roadster for groceries and run into snow on Banta Flats. They were "stuck." They had walked to the Sylvester place to telephone, so would the M.M. and his brother Wallace bring a sled and four horses and come to their aid? Of course they would, but they hooted at "sled and four horses!"

"Clayt's being real funny!" said the mountain man.

They got out the team and a spring-wagon, and Ray decided to take his saddle horse Paderewski, a chunky, husky bay that had often pulled cars through difficulties.

The night was "dark as the inside of a cow," as Mrs. Ryus used to say, so as a sort of concession they took along a lantern - I mean a coal-oil lantern, for if flashlights had been invented at that time they were only for the idle rich.

By the time they were off, it was snowing persistently and the ground was white. It was about seven o'clock. I set a pot of soup to simmering, for I knew Clayt and Red would be hungry, tired and maybe wet. I stoked the range with good old aspen wood and went to the living room to wait and to grade some grammar papers. An hour went by. I looked at the clock, arose, went to the kitchen, put in another stick of wood, opened the door, and stepped out onto the porch. A wall of white was all I could see. I listened. Yes, faint and far away, came the sound of a laboring motor. I came back, stirred the soup and got out clean towels. Then I went out again. Yes, I could still hear the motor - quite remarkable how far sound carries sometimes! Back I went to my papers. I looked at the clock - nine. Back to the kitchen, put in another stick of wood, stirred the soup, went outside again. Still that motor - no nearer and no farther. It was very funny, and not "ha-ha funny" either. Then inside again, I sat, stoked the stove, stirred the soup, and just sat until twelve-thirty.

Ray came in on Paderewski first, followed in about thirty minutes by Wallace with the team and wagon and the two men - hungry, tired and very wet. Wal's only comment was that the two-horse team was all right, but he wished he'd taken a sled.

It seemed that they had found the snow falling heavily when they had left the ranch, and visibility was zero. Ray had led his horse while trying to find the highway by locating telephone poles; then he accidentally knocked the lantern against a rock, which ended any assistance from that article. At long last, they reached the car. I do not know how deep the snow was then, but Clayt said there had been a foot of snow at the car when they had "stuck."

The next morning the snow measured exactly forty-eight inches here in our yard - level with the top of the fence! Cattle had to be fed. Out with the team and bobsled and hayrack they went. The cattle had evidently been as surprised as we at the suddenness of the winter. They were scattered practically all over the meadow, and so bemused they stood like statues looking dazedly through snowy lashes, rather than starting an immediate trek to the feed sled. Ray had to come back for his horse, ride out, and drive them to the hay.

We had been invited to the Workman ranch a quarter of a mile below for dinner. I called Mrs. Workman and told her I knew we could not make it, as doubtless the boys would be very late getting the feeding done. She reminded me that we would have to pass by when we fed our bulls at the Roberts' place. She said she had roasted two hens; and we could have our meal en route home from Roberts'. It was a Thanksgiving Day to be remembered!

There are places in the pastures along the river that are known as "sloughs," though Emma McCrone has, to my mind, a far better name for these morasses of boggy hummocks of grass resting on, and surrounded by, black oozy mud and water. She calls them "hummy-loopers," in the phraseology of the cowboy, for a loop you can be thrown while traversing such terra infirma! Never did I become so adept in crossing that I failed to get at least one foot a mess.

One sunny morning in late June, attired in a ruffled - and, for heaven's sake, white dress with white hose and baby-doll patent-leather shoes, circa 1920 - I decided to walk to the place where my Mountain Man was constructing a raft to use in crossing the river. We had a lot of water in the river in those days, and his team had learned that by staying on the other side their chances of being harnessed and put to work were so much less.

I took the short cut which brought me to a slough. Ray was just across, so I called for him to come and help me over the "hummy-loopers," as he was wont to do. But he answered: "You can make it - just come on."

Well, it seemed the honeymoon was either over or drawing near the end. So I started, stepping gingerly, and - according to Ray's version of this tale - keeping my eyes turned toward the blue sky above. Perhaps I did, invoking aid therefrom. I managed three or four steps, and then fell face down in the muck. Heaven having denied me help, I suppose I concluded to help myself, for somehow I got up and out and across. Wiping the - I think - peat from my eyes, I looked for my lawfully wedded man....who wasn't there!

Further search discovered him rolling 'round in the grass, helpless with laughter.

I went back to the cabin - the long way - to bathe and shampoo the mud, the grass, the tadpoles, and water bugs out of my hair. To this day, I have never learned to negotiate these bogs with anything like the proper equilibrium and/or equanimity.

This was an afternoon! And it lasted into the night. The Wright triumvirate - Wallace, Ray and I - had eaten the midday meal. Wallace went off to walk to the fish hatchery, about a mile and a half north, to feed the little trout he had there; Ray went to his many jobs of this and that about the barns, shops, etc. I was doing the dishes and debating the merits of a walk over Clear Creek way. It was early December, and there was very little snow but a mean little wind was blowing out of the north.

I heard someone calling. It was Ray running toward the barn; and this, along with his yelling and his looking up the road, told me something was amiss. He was trying to attract Wallace's attention, but to no avail. Wallace admitted later that he had heard him but thought nothing of it. Ray was one of those in whom the joy - the very elixir - life was so intense that sometimes it seemed there was no containing it; in fact, it was impossible, except by spontaneous "Wa-hoos!" and "Hi-yos!" When I first became acquainted with this startling though lovable trait, and asked the reason for the yelling, he answered: "Why not? It's too quiet around this place." He went on with another whoop that literally made the welkin resound.

So you see, Wallace's inattention was excusable. What had happened was this: Our cattle, which we keep on the meadows winters and feed with hay from the stacks scattered about, always gather along Crooked Creek and the small lakes -

now ice-covered - built for water storage, to yank and nibble on the slough grass, a coarse, rough sedge. It has little nutritional value but our cows seem to like it; and as long as there is any in sight - i.e., until the snow covers it - they will be found wading out in it up to their chins every afternoon.

Somehow a bunch of them had crowded along the edge of the lower pond nearby, out onto the ice, and had broken through!

There were thirty-three of the poor animals thrashing 'round in the deepest part, and anybody would know they'd have to be gotten out and soon.

In less time than it takes for me to relate this, Ray had his team - good ol' Duke and Joe - harnessed, the woven wire fence along the dam cut and removed, and was "snaking" cows out of the "drink." He'd first throw a rope around their necks, of course, as they floated near the dam.

So much happened so quickly, and we were so engrossed in the work, that I am rather vague about some of it, especially my part. I know that sometimes I drove the team, sometimes handled the ropes, giving them to Ray at strategic moments, or ran back to the barn for more when one broke or when we had to leave it on one of the "old sisters," or "blisters," as Ray called them, when one refused to let us remove it. They are gentle cows, almost pets, since we no longer graze them on open range but keep them in our own pastures at the Lower Ranch during summers. Except when we get them into close quarters! I think Herefords are worse than any other breed about this. Brother! Can they ever "get-on-the-fight," as cattlemen put it! I had to take to the top rail several times during the melee.

After what seemed an age, we had all out but one. This was an old milk cow. She was black, with a sort of brownish mottled face, and was the pet of the place. Poor old girl! She looked sorry, indeed, her hide soaked through. Somehow she had let the other cattle push her aside as they drifted to Ray's rope and rescue. "A goner, probably," Ray said. We drew her out onto the bank, where she lay quietly while the rope was taken off, and then she still lay there, shivering and wheezing.

By this time I was having the usual reaction from the long tenseness, and I began flipping with thumb and forefinger some tears from somewhere. Ray ejaculated: "Now, don't you bawl!" and went to get the boulder float, a sheet-metal covered article used in hauling rock, etc.

We - I cannot think what I did except hold Duke's and Joe's lines and flip tears! - managed to get old Ebony onto the float and took her into the barn. There, with pieces of burlap sacks and such, we gave her a rubdown to end all rubdowns. Later, when Wallace had returned and the evening meal was over, we took a lantern and went back to the barn to do more massaging. Lo! Ebony was on her feet and pulling hay out of a manger with a vengeance, as only an old milk cow can do! She survived, and lived on for many years afterward.

Tonight when the kitchen was filled to capacity, as usual, with the overflow sitting in the dining room, and I at my typewriter answering the day's correspondence and the rest occupying chairs, stairs and floor space, "Juicy" Owen remarked that surely there must be some newcomers - he really said "victims" - who hadn't heard the Packer story.

Response was immediate. "I have, but not for ages - besides Miss X hasn't, I'll bet, and maybe Susan." Miss X was a reserved but pleasant type from Vermont, dean of women at a college Susan attended.

So Juicy began the tale - "With your assistance, Mabel" - of Alfred Packer, who slew five companions - history says all of them were Democrats—beside the little crystal stream above Lake City, in Hinsdale County, Colorado, and ate of their flesh, thus giving him meat to tide him over until weather and snow conditions permitted him to get to the Los Pinos Indian Agency post for vegetables. It is a gruesome tale, and even I, who grew up in the shadow of the same mountains that looked down upon the scene of savagery, and have heard the story from cradle days, find it so.

"And when spring came, Packer was seen stumbling along the trail to the Agency doors" -Juicy; ". . . With a leg, they think, belonging to the youngest of the five, over his shoulder, at which he nibbled from time to time" - Mabel.

At this point, poor Miss X, who had been staring in horror as our tale unfolded, began turning a greenish hue about the lips and muttering something. "Excuse me," she said, and left the kitchen. Susan followed in concern, and next morning told me that Miss X was much ashamed of her squeamishness, especially since she "knew" there wasn't even a modicum of truth in the entire yarn!

Anent this: I know a grandmother - Truda McLarty - who uses this as a bedtime story for her many grandchildren. They clamor: "Tell us about the man that ate the five dead muskrats, please Trudie!"

The Mountain Man was engaged in a fence-building project across the Rio Grande at the Lower Ranch. At this specific time he was being assisted by "Vic" Miller, a lad of around eighteen years and one of the group known to us as "the boys," who periodically helped us with the hay harvest, usually starting as sulky-rake operators in the days when teams were in order.

It was just past the middle of June, and a belated spring with cold nights and cool days had slowed the melting of the snow in the high country. Now the weather had turned warmer and summer had arrived suddenly and unheralded. Down came in wild recklessness the deep snows of December and January, swelling the old Rio Grande to astounding proportions, too big for its bridges, and causing doubt whether it would be contained within its legal banks.

Ray and Vic started out as usual in a spring wagon drawn by the husky bays - Strip and Baldy - with tools for the job and lunch bucket, as it was too far to return for the noon meal at the ranch house.

Upon arrival at their usual fording place at the river, Ray remarked: "She's up and will really be rolling by this evening if it is as warm today as it was yesterday; but we'll not worry about that little thing now." Across they went, as usual, the horses churning the water as they negotiated the polished, mobile river boulders, the spray flying high and raining down on beasts and men.

It was hot in the sun and warm in the shade throughout the day; but the fence work went on in normal fashion and with satisfaction to the two workmen. Good men enjoy building a good fence, I've noted in my long career.

Quitting time came with the sun low in the sky, and soon its rays would be shut off by the mountain that looms high at that part of our ranch. By the time the team had been hitched to the wagon and they were ready to go, a little breeze laden with a bit of leftover winter chill came up, and both fellows put on their jackets.

When they reached the ford, I think even Ray was surprised at the extent the river had risen since morning. He voiced this to Vic and expressed a bit of doubt as to the feasibility of making a crossing. "But it is a hell of a way to the bridge and around that way!" Vic agreed that it "Shore is!"

Ray decided, if Vic was willing, to try to cross. I suppose youth had something to do with it, but Ray was ever the sort to take a chance, and would always rather be killed by a single blow than hacked to pieces with a table knife any day. Vic was of similar persuasion.

So they made preparations. The fence-building tools were wired together, and the whole to the wagon seat. Vic held the big galvanized pail which held their lunch utensils, including a quart-sized thermos bottle - a Stanley, one of the first steel- jacketed unbreakables.

They climbed in and seated themselves and were off down the bank and into the water. Naturally, they expected water to come into the wagon and to have to draw their feet up and brace themselves against the dashboard. But they were not to mid-stream - the horses swimming with heads high - when Ray knew the score. He shouted to Vic: "This outfit is gonna flip and we'll have to jump." Then: "Jump, boy! Just as far as you can!"

Jump they did, just as the current picked the wagon up like a cracker box and turned it over. Ray caught a glimpse of Vic in mid-air, his coat fanning out and above his head and the lunch pail making a parabola.

The horses drew the wagon and Ray on out onto the bank. He turned to look, and there was Vic swimming like a duck but being borne by the current back to the shore from which they'd come. Yelling above the tumult of the waters, Ray admonished him, "Come back here! I'm not going to make another trip over there for you." Vic managed to turn and swam out. Ray, giving him a hand up the bank, said: "Kid, I never thought to ask you if you could swim when I told you to jump!" Vic replied: "I didn't know - I never tried before!"

They drove home and regaled us with the story of their adventures. I recall one special attribute of the whole affair: one lone dry spot about the size of a silver dollar on the back of the collar of Ray's blue chambray shirt. How or why it was there I'll never understand, for even their hair was dripping!

When I expressed horror at what might have happened to them, they would only look at each other and laugh. Well, as the Mountain Man so often said: "You only live once, but if you go at it right, once is enough!"

We never learned what became of the pail and the thermos bottle. Possibly some little brown boy picked them up at Brownsville, Texas!

Part I

In this tale, the old adage about ignorance being bliss is applicable; or, as Ray puts it: "The fellow who doesn't know applesauce from wild honey has the best time!"

Harry Frye, the big, handsome Georgian, with his soft and beguiling "Gawga" accent, had a troublesome time fishing in the Rio Grande at the Lower Ranch one night.

To begin with, the evening was one without a moon, and even the stars seemed more remote and less helpful than usual. The willows and brush along the stream snagged person and tackle in veritable witchery. Even the river boulders seemed slipperier.

Harry had finally established himself just short of midstream in a favorable fishing spot and was happily casting the special fly of the hour over the water. Aside from the sound of the rippling stream, the voice of a cow in the pasture as she spoke occasionally to her calf, and the lonely sound of a nighthawk going about his business, all was still. Harry was alone, as his fishing partner had gone at least a quarter of a mile away to do his fishing.

Suddenly, there came a loud and startling: "Plop! Plop! Plop!" It came from nearby; and the waters, in which Harry stood in frozen quietude, rippled noisily. Then, horrors! Something dark, solid and very much alive swam right between his legs and on downstream.

The thought of alligators did not help, because common sense discounted this - there couldn't be " 'gators" as far "nawth" as this! "But what kind of mountain boomah was it?" demanded our Harry upon his precipitate arrival at headquarters.

"Only a beaver," Wallace answered; and, of course, that is exactly what it was. However, we agreed that the experience had been very hair-raising to Harry, and we all properly commiserated with him.

Part II

The very next afternoon, after a morning of successful fishing in the same portion of the river where the beaver had disturbed him the evening before, Harry decided naps were for the ladies and the old and decrepit, and drove over into the Clear Creek country. He said afterward that his experience with the beaver had aroused his curiosity; and there being a number of them in that area, with their numerous ponds and odd houses, he was desirous of obtaining more knowledge of the creatures.

As anticipated, he found the dams of the small lakes and their homes very interesting. Beaver dams are marvels of construction, with the surface neatly and compactly tamped by those same flat tails whose plopping on the water has startled many of us.

He saw no beaver, of course, as they are nocturnal in their habits. After a while, he turned to other matters, which were - of all the alls! - two black bear cubs! Quite as aroused as he, they obeyed the teaching of their mother, who was not in sight, and immediately climbed a fair-sized aspen tree.

Harry was intrigued by the funny, fat lil' "boogers" and began tossing small rocks at them, hoping to get them to come down from the tree. But they did not come, continuing to hold fast to their perches, their bright little shoe-button eyes fixed on this strange two-legged intruder.

This exciting episode, the second in less than twenty-four hours, was quite enough for Harry, who rushed back to the ranch and gave some fifteen or so of us in the kitchen his colorful version of his latest experience.

After he had gone to his cabin, we all looked at each other. Ray laughed and said: "That Harry! Run from a beaver and throw rocks at cub bear! If one of 'em had even squeaked, their momma'd soon have made mincemeat of the 'son-of-Gawga'!"

For, of course, she had been in the bushes only a few feet away, watching the play.

The Lost Is Found

The Scandinavian trio, Frank Lief, Otto Anderson and Adolph Johnson, of Cabin Number 2, walked over the hill - about a quarter of a mile - to fish Clear Creek in the afternoon. It was a mild, sunny day in October, and the water just right. As all good sportsmen do, they separated, each taking a stretch of the creek and keeping a suitable distance from the others. Casting where another is fishing is a lapse of good manners, and nothing is more unpardonable in the angler's world.

They fished leisurely - Anderson was seventy and the other two nearing that - crisscrossing the creek for a matter of hours, until the sun nearing the western horizon and a little breeze that had sprung up reminded them that, after all, this was October, and the cool-to-cold night would be coming on.

Frank and Adolph clambered up the bank at about the same time. They discussed their luck and agreed it was time they were getting back. They waited a bit for Otto - "Saw him at the bend below, maybe a half-hour ago; he'll be here soon." Finally, Adolph, who had a voice that made the hills resound, tried shouting for the errant fisherman. No answer. "Ve yust go on. He is grown up."

So they came back to the cabin. They busied themselves getting wood and kindling chopped, building a rousing fire in the cabin range, and making preparations for supper. Adolph was the designated cook; and while he fried sausage, fried potatoes, made up a batch of biscuits, and fixed the coffee, Frank set the table and opened up a can of tomatoes - the bachelor's salad in these parts.

Neither man talked much, but Adolph was the charier of speech of the two. Frank, from time to time, questioned why "that dum' faller" didn't get on in. Adolph, engrossed with his work, was not disturbed: "Oh, he come - you see!"

They heard the light plant at the Big House start, and Frank snapped the light on. This, and the fact that he had the meal ready, startled Adolph into looking at his watch. "Six o'clock! Almost dark! What in the world can be keeping old Otto, anyway!"

Both men went outside and scanned the hill across the highway. All was still save for the muffled put-put of the Delco motor at the house. Bristol Head was a purple-black mass in the east, faintly outlined by the afterglow of the setting sun. It was that lonely, strange time of evening - too light to be dark and too dark to be light. Only two stars had appeared.

With one accord, and in silence, the two men crossed the road and began climbing the hill. At the top, at a spot permitting them to look down on the creek, they rested. Adolph called: "Ott-o-o-o!" several times, both listening intently after each call. No reply. No sound, except for the soughing of the wind in the trees along the creek and the cry of a nightbird, or "bullbat," as we call it.

By this time it was definitely night and the stars were out. A faint glow at the right of Bristol foretold the rising of the full moon. Frank commented that the latter would be a help. Both knew now that something had definitely gone wrong with Otto and that they must have aid in the matter. I don't know why they had not gone to the house and told us of the circumstances in the beginning; but knowing these people, I think they felt it was their problem as long as they had any hopes whatever of solving it themselves. There are people even in these days who feel the same way - that "every tub ought to stand on its own bottom," as our grandmothers said.

Back they came to our house and explained the affair to us. We had just finished our evening meal, and the three Wright men - Wallace, Ray and Warren - at once began putting on hats and light jackets. Gathering up flashlights, they were off to search the banks of Clear Creek, accompanied by Frank and Adolph.

Cecil and I kept up a rather brisk conversation as we did the dishes, commenting on the ifs, ands, and buts of the situation, while the children stood about with wondering eyes. I remember Jean's asking: "Aunt Mabel, did Misser Anderson fall in the water and will be drown-dead when they fine him?"

Time passed. The children were put to bed, but we sat around idly, unable to settle down to knitting or even reading with any kind of satisfaction. Occasionally, we would go outside and look toward Clear Creek and listen. The moon was up and flooding the landscape with silvery light making every tree and big rock on the hill across the way stand out in sharp relief.

Hours later, the men returned without having seen a trace of Otto. We were nonplused. As for Adolph and Frank, I think they were also confounded, though "stoical" seemed to describe their attitude better. "Ve vait 'til tomorrow."

We all slept, I suppose - I am sure I did, as I always do! - but we awakened early with heavy hearts, for subconsciously we had no hopes that the wanderer had returned during the night. A check with his two friends disclosed that he had not. Poor fellows! They looked worn and sad.

As soon as a hurried breakfast was over, we met on the open south porch of the kitchen to discuss plans. We must telephone the neighbors; for, few though they were, all would help. We had been there but minutes when we heard the sound of a motor down the road, and soon a car appeared. It was Mrs. Wetherill. She stopped at the turnstile, and out of her car stepped . . . Otto!

We sat silently as he walked across the yard to us. I think we were too dazed to speak. Then Frank got up and said, slowly and most distinctly: "Vel! Vere have you been, and vat have you been doing?"

Poor, tired old Otto just gave him a look, but it told volumes! Then, without one word, he turned and, in all dignity, walked back to the cabin!

I laughed, and though no one joined me, I am sure they all felt as I did. Relieved of the anxiety connected with the affair, it seemed somewhat of an anticlimax, this ending.

Later, Adolph gave us the details of Otto's experience. He had gone up the creek, passing both of the other fellows without their knowledge; and as he fished, he had crossed and recrossed the stream several times. When he decided to quit, he crossed to the bank on the ranch side - so he thought!

By the time he realized his mistake, he was up on the ridge - a folded, grassy hill and dotted variously with great rocks that appear to have been strewn about by the hand of a giant.

He was lost - completely; and people who have had this experience tell me that they are overcome by a panicky feeling of utter helplessness. Reason takes wings!

Something of the sort happened to Otto. He wandered first this way and then that, but evidently not in a true circle, as he said he did not climb higher nor did he go lower. He would stop to rest from time to time, sitting huddled in his light jacket on one of the big rocks. After night came on, he said he could see the lights of the cars as they traveled the highway below. But still he seemed unable to reason logically and to walk downward. Perhaps he thought it farther than it really was; but anyway, he continued to wander, occasionally sitting to rest, until the night chill forced him to travel again, back and forth, forth and back. Poor old man!

When morning came, he seemed to be more composed - his senses returned, he said - and he used some sound judgment. He started walking down toward the highway and reached it this side of Seepage Creek, where Mrs. Wetherill, en route to Creede, picked him up and brought him to us.

It was an experience that we all felt we could do without. I think Otto and his pals felt so too, for they went back to Colorado Springs and, to date, have not returned to this country.

For several years, the summer guests have included a contingent of Santa Fe Railroad officials, including the general superintendent. Among them at this time were Bert Class, and a Carson, and, of course, our own - retired and spending the full season - "Uncle Charlie," Charles R. Gilfillan, former livestock agent from Kansas City, Missouri.

Messrs. Class and Carson - dears both of them, but, of course, typical of the breed, exact to the nth degree or, as it is put colloquially, "cranky" - occupied Cabin Number 8.

Uncle C. had his usual quarters in the ranch house. It was his custom to arise early while the frost was still on the pump out front, where he always hied for a jug of fresh cold water and, I vow, held his hands under the spout for thirty minutes to insure proper coolness. Then he would place them on the necks of us kitchen folks, who, though knowing what would ensue, nevertheless could not forbear from emitting startled shrieks. Those ice-cold hands! His heart was as warm accordingly, I am sure.

Knowing that the two gentlemen in Cabin Number 8 were unaccustomed to our chilly mornings, and also novices at building wood fires, Uncle Charlie would go to their cabin, build a rousing fire in the stove, put a teakettle of water on for their morning ablutions, and then leave, permitting them to dress in warm comfort.

I am forgetting to mention that Uncle Charlie was a practical joker, full of pranks and tricky doings. This particular morning he happened to note the teeth of Class and Carson - both wore dentures - reposing in their separate receptacles on the shelves of the cabin walls, one on the east, one on the west.

It was easily done. The two abed were sleepily grumpy, complaining about the chill of the morning and, doubtless, about the ungodly earliness of the breakfast hour at Wrights' Ranch. Certainly they opened not their eyes while Uncle Charlie made the exchange of the dental plates and was off.

Chuckling with glee, he encountered Ray Wright, and the two of them hid around the corner of Number 7 to await developments. Outside came Class and Carson to take a look at the day, prognosticate the fishing, and don their teeth. Class was the first to splutter, gag and mutter as to what in blankety-blank ailed these blankety teeth. "Can't get the blankety-blanks in my mouth!" Almost at once, Carson began like sputtering: "Mine neither. What in the blank is wrong? Hey, you old goat!

You've got my teeth!" "Well, you've got mine, blast it all!" Then, practically in unison, "That blankety Charlie Gilfillan!"

Then the audience of two appeared and disappeared as fast as they were able, weak with laughter, for the house and breakfast.

At the Workman ranch house, formerly the old Texas Club, it was late autumn. The day which had been sunny and pleasant was ending; and, as is often the case at this season of the year, the air was becoming chilly and would be downright cold less than an hour after sunset.

The evening chores were done systematically but as speedily as possible - no tarrying about the milking, looking over the corral fence at the landscape, thinking long, long thoughts of things not of the moment, as boys will do; and no lingering about the barn, rubbing the horses' noses and talking to the colts.

At dusk, with the lamps lighted - just coal-oil lamps but with the mellow radiance Mother Workman's polished lamps always gave - they were all gathered in the big kitchen, awaiting the evening meal which Mrs. Workman was preparing.

Father Workman sat beside the huge wood-burning range, puffing on his corncob pipe filled with "long green" ordered direct from Kentucky - relaxed, resting from the day's labor.

Tom and Carl each had a book - Chip of the Flying U, for one, I'd bet, and win!

Little Emmett sat near his brothers beside the table, engrossed with a toy bank, a gift on his lately passed fourth birthday. It was a most ingenious affair of brightly painted metal fashioned into a log cabin—"Uncle Tom's Cabin," with Uncle Tom at the door, one foot extended. The trick was this: a coin placed on the toe of Uncle Tom's boot would be kicked by a hidden spring arrangement up and back into the widemouthed chimney of the cabin.

There was the pleasing jingle of money as Emmett moved the toy about in play. He'd exhausted the supply of small coins supplied by his elders long before this; but anyway, he had "money in the bank," as he proudly put it.

"You shoulda had your birthday earlier, kid," said his brother Tom, looking up from his reading, "so's the tourists could have contributed. It's too late in the season for anybody now."

The words had scarcely been spoken when the two dogs outside set up a barking, and minutes later there was a knock at the door. Mrs. Workman opened it wide to disclose a tall stranger garbed in the everyday wear of men who must brave the outdoors in our mountainous clime.

"Good evening" was exchanged, and the caller requested lodging for himself and his saddle horse, whose reins he held in his left hand. "Certainly, mister." Then, turning her head, she called, "Carl!" Without further words, Carl arose, put on his jacket and Stetson, and accompanied the stranger to take care of his horse.

"He won't need to be watered - he drank a barrel down the road a piece," said the man. Soon both men were back inside the warm, cozy kitchen.

"Show the gentleman his room, Carl. The one at the head of the stairs will be the most comfortable. Then both of you come to supper."

After washing his hands and dabbing a bit at face and hair, the man was seated and the meal began. There was only desultory conversation while they ate. After they had finished, the man became more talkative, perhaps because of Mrs. Workman's most excellent cooking; and in the course of events, he addressed himself to Emmett, whose round blue eyes had been watching his every movement.

Shortly, the little boy produced his bank, explaining: "I got it for my birthday!" Details of its operation were given, and the stranger deposited a coin as directed. Into the bank Uncle Tom kicked the coin. It was a fascinating business, and soon the man had emptied his pockets of coins. Turning to Mrs. Workman, he asked her if she could give him change for a twenty-dollar bill. She assented and asked: "All in coins?" "All," he replied and the fellow spent the next forty minutes or so gleefully watching the money fly into the bank. It would have been hard to determine which of the two, man or boy, enjoyed the play most. Both were quite hilarious, the man's laugh booming out along with the chortles and giggles of the child.

But at last the bank was full to the top, and the stranger indicated that bed was his next move. He paid Mrs.

Workman for the accommodations, saying that he had a long way to go and possibly would arise early and be off before any of the family were up.

I doubt whether the family in the kitchen made even a passing comment on their guest, not even about his not once mentioning his name. Strangers were not new to this place, where many a weary traveler through the years had found food and rest. I have often thought of Mrs. Workman as the woman described in the Bible whose price was far above rubies; and I doubt not but that she has now found her reward - God rest her soul!

An hour later, as the family - minus Emmett, who was tucked away in his trundle bed - was still gathered in the kitchen, the dogs began another clamor, and the sounds of horses' feet and voices of men were heard.

Tom, remarking that business seemed to be rushing tonight, opened the door wide to Frank Soward, the local sheriff, with a posse of three.

Soward explained that they were looking for a man who had held up a saloon in Alamosa early that day, killed the bartender and escaped, presumably up the river. In fact, he'd been seen at Wagon Wheel Gap, or so it had been reported.

In the midst of all this, while the dogs continued their uproar, and while the entire party was congregated outside the house, into their midst, and virtually atop those still in their saddles, the stranger dropped from the upper porch roof! He was clothed as though he had never been abed. I think he may have made an effort to take one of the horses, but if so he failed and by the time any order had been established amidst the hullabaloo, he was off and away afoot. Carl said the last he saw of the man, he was running back of the barns, apparently for the Big Ridge, a terrain of steep humps and hollows with great rocks dotting it here and there.

It was pitch-dark - no moon - and I suppose the officers felt that their quarry afoot would have little chance of escaping them, so they decided to spend the night and take up the chase at daybreak next morning.

Among details given the Workmans was that, after the shooting, the stranger tried to pull a diamond ring off the finger of the bartender; and, failing in this, he drew out a knife, cut off the finger, and put it, ring and all, into his jacket pocket.

They found him the next afternoon, haggard and meek. In fact, he walked out from behind a rock with his hands above his head in mute surrender. The finger and diamond ring were still in his pocket!

I am happy to state that little Emmett never learned of the sad ending that came to his friend.

On a small but picturesque ranchstead up one of our creeks there dwelt for many years a man known to all save, perhaps, the census taker, as "Turnip." Do not ask me why, for I do not know. Perhaps in the dim past he had wrested a living of a sort from truck gardening.

However, when I first heard of Turnip, his livelihood stemmed from an entirely different source. He was a moonshiner - i.e., he operated a still, making com, potato, or whatever sort of whiskey. This was in Prohibition days, and I think he had no trouble selling his product. Turnip made good whiskey; but more about this later.

There was the rumor, widely circulated, that Turnip was one of those who embrace occultism. He dreamed strange dreams, saw visions of things not of this world. In short, as the neighbors put it, he was "batty as a bedbug."

Once in a while, a new tale of some of Turnip's dealings or experiences with the supernatural would reach my ears. He lived alone. On occasion, some daring fellow would "spend the winter" with him -but in a separate cabin. Turnip was left strictly alone in his house with his ghosts.

One spring, a young man in the neighborhood arranged to plant lettuce on a share basis on Turnip's place. It was coming along fine, about ready for cutting, and the price was good. But the young man did not harvest the crop. He left it all for Turnip and met inquiries with the terse statement that he wouldn't be caught dead on the place. I think he meant that he was afraid he would be caught dead there!

Time passed. One day in early spring, I was returning home from one of my rare trips "out." I was the sole passenger on the bus until Del Norte, when a man entered, giving a nod to the bus driver and receiving similar acknowledgment from him. The man took a seat opposite me.

He was tall, well proportioned, with the ruddy complexion that comes of outdoor living; and he was dressed in the usual corduroy trousers, denim shirt, leather jacket, Stetson hat.

Now, all along the highway from South Fork up, at this season of the year, one may see deer and elk; and regardless of how often or how many you may see, there is something about these creatures of the wild that never fails to thrill. This morning was no exception, and several bands of them, numbering from three or four to a dozen, were sighted.

Soon the man across the aisle and I were carrying on a conversation. He was very interesting, telling me of this and that regarding the country, the game, etc. Something gave me a clue as to his identity, and I asked: "Aren't you Turnip?" He was, indeed!

I thought how ridiculous were the ways of idle rumor and gossip! There was positively nothing wrong with the man. He was very intelligent, and his blue eyes shone as kindly and as sane as any man's.

There was a lull in our conversation—I probably had to stop to catch a breath. Suddenly, Mr. Turnip said in an odd tone: "Well, it is coming fast!" And, at my inquiring look, he stated: "You know, don't you, this earth is only half ours? Originally, it was a complete globe, but was split by Divine Power. We inhabit the flat surface of our half. The other is revolving in space and, eventually, will join us."

Aghast, I managed a feeble: "But what will happen to us?"

"Ah!" replied Turnip, and proceeded with a dissertation on original sin, predestination, and utter damnation!

"Well!" I thought. And believe it or not, I spoke not another word during the remainder of the trip. Now I knew! And I, certainly, would have left him the lettuce crop, too!

About Turnip's moonshine business - I stated before that it was a thriving one. The "revenue" men tried almost continually for months to catch up with him, but never did. They were "outsmarted" from the very beginning.

It was small wonder that they never located the still, for Turnip, after making up what he decided would be enough liquor for the duration of the Prohibition era, simply destroyed it. He took the necessary precautions in the sale of his goods. As to where and how he hid them, I shall never divulge the secret. It was such a cunning, ingenious, out-and-out brilliant plan! And, after all, who knows what hard times may come my way!

It is deep winter in January, 1952. The snow measures forty-two inches on the meadow. Although for weeks we have seldom failed to get from three to eight inches every night, the depth on the meadow, like the laws of the Medes and Persians, altereth not.

Scarcely a morning but poor Ray has to shovel snow off the haystack and haul it out of the yard - no place to put it inside - before getting hay for the cattle feeding. As for maintaining any kind of a satisfactory sled road -well, he has abandoned all hope of that.

Each evening when supper is over and I've done the dishes, the triumvirate - Wallace, Ray and I - sit down to play canasta. I sometimes win a game, though Wallace never can understand how I do it - "No card sense whatever!"

At exactly eight-thirty by the old Seth Thomas on the shelf, Ray and I prepare to go on an "Elk Spook." With help from both men, I am made ready. First, I don over my cotton anklets a pair of white wool athletic socks of Wallace's - he has dozens of pairs, gifts from a friendly basketball coach. Since Wallace wears a size-ten shoe, the socks fit me adequately plus and come up cozily above my ankles. Next come a pair of felt bedroom shoes and my rubber galoshes with four buckles - the warmest footwear combination I have ever tried. In fact, I doubt that my feet could ever be cold when so dressed.

Then I stand on the kitchen table while Ray ties my jeans around my ankles, over the galoshes, with stout cord. My heavy, lined leather jacket zipped up, a pink wool scarf on my head, and lamb's-wool-lined mittens, and we are off!

I carry a powerful flashlight - lantern type with a bail handle - while Ray has a thirty-thirty rifle.

It is probably snowing, and the night is ink-black. We walk down through the barn lot, across the Crooked Creek bridge at the dam of the ice-stilled pond, and through the feed lot where the yearlings are lying in groups around the pens. The docile creatures scarcely stir, just blink snow-fringed lashes at us as we pass to the gateway leading to the meadow and oblivion! Here is where the fun (?) begins.

We walk single file, first Ray, then I, shining the light ahead on the track of the sled road. Ray seems instinctively able to follow this road, even without the light. But I - alack and alas! I waver and stumble and can go but a short way before I step off the hard-packed trail into snow that comes right up under my armpits. Ray waits patiently while I struggle up and out and back onto the path again. He waits not silently but offers remarks in true husbandly fashion: "How do you manage to be so awkward? Even old Star and Pat stay up better'n that, and they have four feet apiece to look after! Do you want me to carry that lantern? . . ."

No answer, for after a dozen or so falls, I am too angry to speak -and for me this is something! I become so disgusted and so exhausted from my struggles along the quarter- to half-mile we traverse, I doubt whether I'd have made any effort to right myself had I not been so boiling mad!

By this time we have neared the haystack from which Ray is feeding at this time - thank Heaven the stacks farther away are paneled against the marauders!

I shine the flashlight toward the stack, Ray lifts his rifle and, pointing it up-country, fires. The sound echoes and re-echoes from the surrounding hills but seldom dies before we hear our elk. That is, if there are any in the hay tonight. There are cracking, popping sounds as they go over the stackyard fence or gates. On occasion, they run past us so close I can imagine their breath on my cheeks. They take huge leaps over and through the snow, leaving holes large enough to bury a piano. They are "spooked!"

We turn and make our way back; and, strange to relate, I seem to be able to negotiate the roadway much better on the return trip, committing, perhaps, only one or two faux pas!

We walk around each pen to see that no foolish calf has, in his greed, fallen on his back in the racks. In case of such an accident, he must be helped out soon, or the result can be disastrous.

We manage amiable conversation as we go, commenting on the snow -after all, it is needed if we are to have a hay crop next summer, etc. Ray says: "All the San Luis Valley farmers will be wearing grins like waves on a slop bucket this spring!"

All's well! The light from the kitchen windows beams a welcome. We are home!

Many great and wonderful things have happened to me and one of the greatest is the privilege of becoming a part of this special piece of earth - the Upper Rio Grande country!

In 1916, you could teach school if you passed "Teachers' Tests" which meant tests in a series of subjects, issued by the Colorado State Superintendent of Schools. These were given under supervision of the local superintendent. A certificate or license to teach would then be issued: First, Second or Third, according to the "grade" you made, except that, though a rating of 90% was attained as required for a "First," you had to have had several months of teaching experience before you would be issued anything other than a Second Grade Certificate. Also, you were supposed to be eighteen years old for either grade, though this was sometimes tacitly ignored, as it was in my case.

Personal family circumstances required that after graduating from high school, I get a job. So I took the State Tests and passed them with a grade of 91%. In those days, I had a lot of confidence in me and I was not at all surprised. At fifteen, I had thought I knew everything worth knowing, and at sixteen I was sure of it. At seventeen, I was less sure.

There was a little summer school in our county at Hermit Lakes in need of a teacher. Since it was in a somewhat isolated region, it had not been too easy to find a teacher willing to accept and stay on the job. For instance, one of the Lake City young women who had taught part of a term at Hermit, warned me that it was too lonely for words and that I'd "just die" if I went there. I was not perturbed, never having been really lonely in my life.

My people had a ranch about eight miles north of Lake City, and as my mother could not conveniently move into town for the school term - she did so just once to my knowledge - I was "boarded out" in private homes and thus sent to school.

The town was like a big family to me. There was scarcely a pantry in the place to which I did not feel free to go if I were hungry.

Sometimes I would go home Saturday mornings on the little narrow gauge train that ran down the Lake Fork canyon six days a week. I would stop at the High Bridge - that marvelous structure of wood, four hundred thirty-five feet spanning the gorge, a hundred twenty-five feet above the stream - and the brake- man or the conductor would set me off at our lower meadows, about a quarter of a mile from the ranch house. If Father was too busy to take me back to Lake City by buckboard and team Sunday afternoon, I'd miss a day of school by taking the train Monday evenings. I well remember the thrill of standing beside the track (or right on it!) until Pete Ready, the engineer, recognized my presence by a toot from the engine. He had already slowed the train before crossing the Bridge so could come to a stop with ease. I'd be picked up and taken on the Lake City. One night during the winter of my first year in school, the girls from Grandma McKay's were late in meeting the train. It was dark and I was uncertain as to which way to go, when I spied a group of young men among whom I recognized one I had seen among the high school students. I ran to him, grabbed him around one leg - couldn't reach an arm -- and demanded he take me to Grandma McKay's. I think he may have been rather startled, but laughed and took my hand and off we went, meeting the Big Girls - Ruth Guffey et al. - about a block down the street.

Throughout my school years I accumulated pseudo-relatives, including a grandfather, Will Hunt, father of my "big sister" Carolyn, in whose home I spent much of my high school years. In fact, without her and her husband, Clarence, Tony Baker and a teacher, H. G. Heath, who believed I could really amount to something, I doubt I would have made it! I don't recall ever being homesick. Everyone was kind and good to me.

When it became known that I intended to qualify for and eventually take the Hermit Lakes school for the summer, such interest was shown by the town in general, as you wouldn't believe! Such counseling and advice! Especially do I remember Tony Baker's role in this.

Tony was a sort of self-appointed big brother and served in loco parentis at public affairs where I was present, these being mainly dances held in the old Armory, which was a community building. Dances made up practically the only recreation other than school parties.

I cannot remember when I did not know Tony. My mother and father were married in the Baker home and Mrs. Baker served as a second mother or sometimes grandmother to me. The ranches were just two miles and a half apart. One incident I recall in particular: I was perhaps nine years old when I ran away to Bakers and asked Mrs. Baker to let me live with them. She shooed her family away, took me on her lap and let me tell about my problem at home. Afterward she talked to me and persuaded me that I must go back. For the first time in my life I was given a sense of responsibility and agreed that she was right. I asked her not to tell anyone about the episode and I feel sure she never did. However, I think Tony knew - maybe he listened! - for when I went out to my pony he was waiting and announced he would ride home with me, which he did. When we arrived, my mother came out and said: "Oh, that's where you were!" I went on in and though she talked a short while with Tony, the affair was never mentioned by any of us. Through the years, Tony was alternately teasing or scolding me. The teasing I really did not mind - probably liked it -- but the scoldings I took sometimes, I'm sorry to say, with less than good grace. There was never any use in arguing - I never got to first base! I once told him he was downright obnoxious and he pounced on the word, declaring it one of my peculiar forms of endearment!

For weeks before my departure to Hermit, he by turn advised and commiserated with me. He said Hermit Lakes was the wildest, most uncivilized place he'd ever been; that my pupils would have to be rounded up, roped and tied like calves in order to get them into the school house; that he should have concentrated on teaching me to rope rather than to dance; that perhaps he should try to find me a good "stock dog," etc., etc., on and on. I laughed at all this, of course, or said: "Nuts! How utterly ridiculous can you be! I am not as foolish as you think. etc.

It was a beautiful early June morning when I started for Hermit, riding the dearest little mare, Firefly. I was accompanied by "Grandpa' Will Hunt who would lead my horse back to Lake City after I had met Bert Bent, who was coming half way with a team and buggy. I ran across a letter recently, dated April 16, 1916, in which Mr. Bent said it would be a great convenience if I could so meet him. My clothing, aside from a few pieces and some toilet articles carried in a bag back of my saddle, had been sent by express two weeks before to Creede, where it was picked up and taken to Hermit.

At almost the last minute we were joined by Aunt Jen Woodruff who needed to pay a visit to their ranch on the Rio Grande about twelve miles below hermit. I do not know why Mr. Woodruff did not accompany us. He may have been ailing as he often was, I think. I really do not remember much about him except that he always called her "Jen" and that he had a rather funny habit, when faced with a problem, of opening his mouth like a giant frog two or three times and smacking his lips before speaking in a deep voice, saying, "Jen, Ahm in Hell's Hole!"

Anyway, we three started out together. After we had left the Lake Fork and were on the road leading on and up the Slumgullion, that massive earthslide that is responsible for beautiful Lake San Cristobal, I was in new territory. We were riding along, Grandpa and I, side by side, with Aunt J. close behind us, when we heard a sudden thud. Aunt Jen had fallen off her horse onto the edge of the road. I don't know which one of us reached her first though I think I did, but after it seemed she was not visibly badly hurt - she said she had felt dizzy and had, apparently, blacked out for an instant - Grandpa decided he must go back to town for Dr. Cummings. There was nothing for me to do but wait and be of as much comfort to Aunt J. as possible. When she remarked that she wished it had all happened nearer water, as she felt terribly thirsty, I immediately got my drinking cup - one of those collapsible things that held just a cup and no more! - and was off down over rocks and brush to the stream, which seems now to have been quite a distance, but at the same time no big deal, though I do remember thinking I'd have to be extremely careful if I were to return with a full cup. However, with my usual luck - 1 am convinced all the stars out at my birth were happily fortuitous - I found an old tomato can. It was rusty but it was of decent size and it held water. I carried it with remarkable success, considering the terrain, to refresh Aunt Jen who seemed to have recovered her usual cheerful self, much to my relief, for truth to tell, I had been "scared to pieces."

Eventually, the doctor arrived in his Model T Ford - one of the first three in Lake City - and almost at the same time Mr. Bent, who said he had felt sure I had been delayed, so he had just come on. Mrs. Woodruff got into the car, Grandpa got onto her horse and, leading mine, they were off to Lake City and I was in the buggy with Mr. Bent on the way to Hermit.

An odd thing, perhaps, but I do not recall even a qualm of any kind at parting with anyone, not even my family at the ranch whom I had left the day before. Not even Grandpa, whom I loved dearly - his stories of experiences in the Civil War had given me my foundation in that history! But, as I said, I was in new territory and entranced!

Bert Bent was a most friendly and interesting person, and at once I discovered we had a common ground - geology. Having been reared in a mining area and accustomed to miners' talk all my life, and having at least a basic understanding of minerals from textbook study, I was eager to listen.

Bert Bent was familiar with Lake City country and its mines - had lived there; his father was buried in the cemetery there; his first wife, a Lake City girl, Eva Morgan, and he, had "prospected" practically all the area through which we were passing. I have known men of many callings and I feel that miners are definitely a special and separate breed. Among no others does one find more zeal and general enthusiasm. The next day, the next round of shots will bring the Bonanza, Kipling has so aptly described the miners' creed:

"One everlasting whisper, day and night repeated so:
Something hidden. Go and find it.
Go and look behind the ranges .
Something lost behind the ranges,
Lost and waiting for you. Go!"

Hermit is about thirty-five miles from Lake City and in a buggy, even if drawn by two horses, as ours was, the trip takes hours, but I was startled when we came to a spot where we could look at the little valley, dotted with lakes, and Mr. Bent pointed it out as "home." In a way it was a dreary scene. Aside from the blue of the lakes, it was a series of flats, dull and drab with patches of willows equally dull - the leaves were out and some early flowers in bloom in Lake City! I think I must have become quiet - had chattered animatedly much of the trip I am sure - for Mr. Bent said he was sure I must be tired and hungry; that we would soon be there; supper would be ready, etc., etc. Shortly, we were.

A log cabin - two large rooms I later discovered - appeared midst the willow clumps with a smaller one next it, below the dam of a lake whose waters were no longer blue but the gray of early twilight. Suddenly I caught a glimpse of a long-legged teen-aged boy before he darted behind a willow cluster. Then there was another youngster and ANOTHER! O, surely not! Surely - I thought - what Tony had said, could not be coming true!

Before I could soar to the zenith or sink to nadir, a door opened and a woman with one of the sweetest faces I ever saw, and with a baby in her arms, came to meet and welcome me.

Once inside, I was given a chair and a glass of water. Then five Bent children - three boys and two girls -- lined up to inspect me -- the baby had been placed in a carriage at one side. I was accustomed to children (goodness knows!), having come from a large family and having often been a "baby sitter," only we called it "stayin' with the kids!" but I must have been somewhat disconcerted, and, for a minute, seemed unable to do anything to relieve the situation. I just sat and stared until one little girl sidled up to me and whispered, "We've got CAKE for supper!" That did it! With an arm around her I went to the carriage and became engrossed with the baby, Dorothy Bent.

There seemed always to be a baby in the Bent family and how clean and sweet they all were! One never hesitated to pick up one of Debby Bent's babies - if they were ever spoiled, they certainly did not smell that way!

When I was able to look about and assess the room, I found it quite large and furnished as dining room-sitting room - also bedroom with a pretty oak bed: mine, I was to learn. There was a long table that could seat eight or eighteen nicely. There were some straight wooden chairs but only three or four. Blocks cut from what must have been a huge aspen log, served for other seats at the table. I was given a chair but soon gave it up for one of the aspen stools. They were light and easily rolled about and they were not hard, though whether softened by time and/or use I know not.

There was a big rocker which I at once guessed as "Papa's," a small couch and a lovely old reed organ. I loved it all. There was a comfortable assurance of contentment and good will permeating the whole. Evenings we would gather around the organ, which Mr. Bent played, and sing.

After our meal, that evening, which was simple and delicious - the rice pudding we had for dessert with the cake was "something," and try as I have, I have never been able to make it as Debby Bent did. The dishes picked up and carried to the kitchen (the "other" room) to be done by the two older boys, Mrs. Bent picked up the baby and prepared to depart to the sleep-cabin next door, the rest of the family having melted away. She placed an extra blanket at the foot of my bed and expressed her wish that I sleep well, said I'd be called in time to dress, etc., before breakfast. Then - bless her! - she leaned and kissed me.

I sat for a time looking out the window at the moon-lit waters of the lake. I could not do without the stars and I would be desolate to some extent without a moon - it does so much for things and people! I sat and realized that for the first time in my life I was away from home among people I had not always known! It was a queer feeling. Was I at my "mature" years going to be homesick? WELL! I thought, I'll just go to bed and sleep and worry about all this tomorrow!

Tomorrow came and from then on I was too busy, too interested, too utterly fascinated and too happy for anything else.

This is how I came to MY COUNTRY.

It was a lovely summer here in this little valley among the Bents, Masons, and Browns, whose children made up my little school. How kind and understanding they all were! I don't think I can ever forget any of it but among notes kept at random - I did not keep a regular diary - I see that I had a difficult time "doing up" my hair. I had seldom worn it in any fashion other than tied with a ribbon, hanging down my back even through high school years, except when one of the girls did it up with pins atop my head. Mrs. Mason sensed my problem at once and suggested I let it hang, at least on Saturdays and Sunday. Bless her!

These people were all engaged in a commercial fish business. They netted trout - mainly Brook - from the lakes, dressed and packed them in ice in special shipping crates and sent them by express from Creede to markets - restaurants and cafes - to Denver.

Fish per se were rare in my life. In fact there had been practically none. There was little fishing done in the Lake Fork until I was half way through high school due to mine waste - mill tailings - being dumped into the stream. There were trout in small lakes about Lake City and in San Cristobal, but these were not easily available to us.

In the fall - October, usually - my father and some of our neighbors would go deer hunting over "on the Blue" - Blue Mesa country. The last day out they would fish and bring back sacks - heavy cotton sacks known as "Seamless" - of little trout - Natives about eight inches long. Mother would fry ours brown and crisp, and we youngsters would eat them practically bones and all. I still like fish but none will ever taste better than those from The Blue!

Still, how delicious those trout we had almost daily at Hermit. The larger fish were ours to eat as the markets at the time wanted smaller ones - three to the pound - since they paid by the pound and one trout per order was served in restaurants and cafes.

There was a spike-nail driven into a log just outside the door of the kitchen cabin of the Masons at Hermit. The fish was hung on this and Luella Mason with her pocket knife - a most excellent utilitarian article with which she could, and did other carving, such as figurines from aspen wood - would make three or four deft slashings and then strip off the skin. The fish would then be laid on a board where it was cut into sections of four or five pieces, depending on the size of the trout. These were dredged with cornmeal or a mixture of flour and cornmeal, previously seasoned, and fried in bacon drippings, or often in butter made by this same Luella. Along with a big bowl of steamed, buttered rice, hot biscuits and honey, here was a meal. While on the subject, I must say that any left over was never wasted, including fish. Mrs. Mason made an especially tasty salad with the meat taken from the bones and mixed with any left-over vegetable - peas, carrots, beans or the like, pickles - and a dressing of thick cream and vinegar. Mm, Mm, good!

Another interesting angle of the fish business was the netting. On Saturdays and some week day evenings, I accompanied Luella Mason - the men being occupied with other tasks - to the landing where the rowboat lay. We'd get in and dispose ourselves, Luella manning the oars, of course. My previous experiences on water in a rowboat had been most unpleasant, and in one instance so hair-raising that none of us involved ever told our parents of the episode, but I never felt the least uneasiness with Luella, though whitecaps covered the waters at times. Rowing out to the spot where the net was set - floats bobbing - we would lift the net (one and three-fourth inch mesh, the size for catching the three-to- the-pound the market required) and take the fish one at a time, dropping them into the boat. It was a thrilling sight, all those beautiful speckled brook-trout, it seemed half a boat full! We had to be careful not to step on them. The fish out, the next step was to tow the net to another spot (anchor-lifted) and reset it. Then back to the landing where some of the men met us and transported the fish by wheelbarrow, generally, to the "dressing" area. Sometimes Luella assisted with this process but I alway seemed to have business elsewhere and after an initial spectatorship, I was convinced this part of the business was not so fascinating. I did watch the packing of the fish in chipped ice in large wooden crates for shipment by express from Creede, thirty miles away. I think that at this time they sold for thirty-five cents per pound. In the beginning, the Hermit Lakers received twenty-five cents per pound. At the end of the marketing business, years later, the price was ninety-five cents.

Before I end my dissertation on trout I'll answer a question I've often been asked: Did you ever fish? Yes, I went with Mr. Mason a few times. He liked to fly-fish evenings. The first time I accompanied him he showed me how to cast and then put the pole in my hand. Almost at once - strictly luck! - I caught a big brook, weighing about three pounds. I drew it up to the boat where Mr. M. was ready to assist me. It was so beautiful, this fish, so full of the joy of life! I was excited at having caught it, but I said, "O, couldn't we let it go!" and that sweet understanding man agreed, removed the hook and the fish slipped away. It was the only one I ever caught though I tried a few other times.

In reference to my teaching duties which, after all, was the purpose of my being at Hermit - all else fringe benefits! - I must say that my experiences in that little school are priceless in my treasury of pleasant memories. I was so very young! Sometimes I wondered who was teaching whom! I was very earnest in my intentions and if I am to take any real credit for my efforts that stammer at Hermit and in other schools later, it lies in any ability I had to instill in my pupils a desire to learn - a thirst for knowledge. Perhaps they already had this but I feel I had a talent for fostering it.

Most of my pupils had known interrupted schooling - had seldom been enrolled at the beginning of a regular term in a town or city school where they had attended and often they had to leave before it ended. But their education had not been neglected even in the winters they sometimes spent at Hermit. The parents saw to this.

The first big snow sealed the family or families in for a long winter. There were many chores. Trails had to be broken to the bam to feed th stock, milk the cows, etc. Apropos the BARN - I always think of it in capitals -- it was a large structure and fascinating to me as all barns are and have been since childhood, but this one held special significance because its shingled roof had known the handiwork of a boy visiting Hermit while on a tour of the West. He was to die while still a boy of eighteen, in the air over France in 1918: Quentin Roosevelt.

Other chores were the ever-lasting wood-cutting, ice to be broken on Mason Creek (known as Carson Creek for years until Rube Fullington renamed it) for water for stock and household, etc., etc. No one was idle.

During the long evenings, in addition to special lessons, there was much reading: classical literature, good magazines, etc., and much profitable discussion of same. The excellent diction of the youngsters impressed me at once.

Considering today's modem schools with the beautiful buildings, unbelievable equipped class rooms, teachers trained for specific teaching, special education classes, etc., that little Hermit Lake school seems incredible! There is another angle and this, I think, the crux of the entire matter - social relationship.

Today there are no town kids and country kids, just KIDS. In my day there was, too often, a difference, a definite prejudice against country children. I was not aware of this at the time but I was one of the lucky ones. I lived in an area where no such caste system prevailed. Today's school buses carry students from one school to another for scholastic meetings, athletic confrontations, etc. There is healthy competition and most important is the socialization - the learning to live with each other. I cannot say that I think schools like that at Hermit are best. I just say they were good.

Debby Bent's Recipe for Rice Pudding - as best I recall it:

Put into a large size, buttered baking dish (no use making a small amount as you'll just wish for more) about two quarts of whole milk. Add a cup of rice. Put into a slow oven for four hours or so. Occasionally stir as a thick "skin" will form -- stir this into the pudding. After cooking almost to the end of the time, add no more than a half a cup of sugar and two teaspoons of vanilla and stir again.

As I have indicated elsewhere, I have never been able to make this so that it tasted as good as Debby's, but it's not bad.

It was Saturday night about six weeks after I came to Hermit. Luella and I were going to pop corn I had run down to the Bents' on an errand of some sort, and returning met several of the fellows who had gathered for the occasion. There were the usual hilarious greetings and badinage, and somebody picked me up, carried me over a small mud puddle and deposited me inside the kitchen door. There to my almost unbelieving eyes sat Tony Baker! I regained speech and mobility simultaneously and was across the room, hugging an arm and demanding how, when and where. I was simply dotty with delight - I who had thought I missed no one from home. Tony must have been surprised at my exuberance though I doubt particularly flattered. Still, there is no telling. He murmured something about having come over to see Fullington about some horses.

There were introductions, etc., and I took the situation over by saying that the corn party should go on and Tony and I would go out to the Open Forum where we could talk and I could find out everything and about everyone at home. The Open Forum was the designation given the pile of old lumber, boxes, wagon - seats, etc., in front of the shop where we younger people often sat in the evenings, discussing and settling the most momentous affairs of the world.

So out Tony and I went - I skipping along, holding onto his arm lest he get away. He used to say that if I hugged the boys' necks as tight as I did his arm, I'd choke them to death! We found a wagon-seat and it went like this:

Mabel: Now talk, Tony- About everyone, but first, how are Mother and the kids? I won't say a word!

Tony: Yeah? Well, I rode by the ranch last week. Mary was in town, the others out somewhere. Your Mother was in her garden. It looks good but it is a lot of work for her.

M: I know, and for the kids, too.

T: She worries about you and --

M: She most certainly does not!

T: Yes, she does. We got to talking and I —

M: Tee-ony Baker! I'll bet you did and you didn't come over here about horses! You and Mother got your heads together and --I'd like to know what you two did in your younger days to always make you so suspicious of me. I have not done one -- by this time I had risen in wrath.

T: Sit down, Fireball, and listen to me. It isn't that you have done anything to worry us, but —

M: Do you mean to tell me that YOU worry about me?

T: I don't know. I think it is like your mother says, you don't or won't ever seem to realize that there is anything wrong or bad in the world. At least you won't see it. I don't think it is because you are so blamed innocent. DAMIFIKNOW, what it is but ever since that time I caught you tryin' to hide --

M: O don't, for heaven's sake, bring that up again! You have absolutely the worst memory of anyone I know - you never forget anything! (THAT refers to a time when I was about four years old and out with my father who was working on an irrigation ditch. I'd been told about the ostrich and its penchant for hiding its head and evidently I was trying to prove something when Tony rode by. How he delighted in telling this story - and at the most unsuitable times:

"There you were, bottom-up, tryin' to bury your head, pink sunbonnet and all, in a pile of sand!").

T: (resuming) You still hide your head. I did tell your mother I'd ride over just to see how you are getting along and --

M: Just dandy! You can see I am!

T: Yeah, I can see that all right. For instance, tonight, those fellows --

M: They are the nicest boys! Why do you always --

T: (sounding real cross) Boys! That fellow packin' you around was a MAN! Migosh, Girl! Don't let them pick you up and fling you around like a rag doll! They aren't the boys you've grown up with!

There was more of this, and then --

M: Please, Tony! Don't scold anymore. I'll be good. I'll be like one of those Hindu people in India - I won't let anyone even touch me!

T: Yes? Well, these people here are all right - that Mrs. Mason is, and anyway you'll be home in another two months. I'll tell your mother you are all right.

M: And tell her, Tony, that one of these fellows is a sheepman and you know I would never love a sheepman!

T: (with a snort) Tell me about your school. Had to rope and tie any of the kids yet?

I gave a good account of experiences including an incident of the day before. We had decided to try filling the cracks between the logs of the schoolhouse with mud to keep out the wind which is chilly even in July at this altitude. I supervised the mixing of the mud and the big boys started chinking, while I busied myself inside. This was the noon hour but we had all eaten our lunches. Suddenly mud balls came flying into the room through the cracks, barely missing the smaller youngsters and me, and I had to run out and stop the fun! For this, the boys had to scrub the floor after school. It needed scrubbing anyway.

Also, one day when I raised the lid of my desk, a water snake reared its head from the chimney of a Log Cabin syrup can and stuck its tongue out at me! "You know how I feel about snakes, Tony!" I know they are harmless but I can't help yelling "Horrors!" when I see one" - and this is the snakiest country!" I reacted satisfactorily for the perpetrators of this deed and Gene Mason took the creature outside and released it.

So we talked - even Tony, a lot for him. Maybe I was a little subdued though I doubt this. It was a beautiful night. The moon wasn't much but all the stars were turned up high and so close I told Tony that if he would boost me up onto the shop roof and hand me a stick, I knew I could reach one or two. But he wouldn't so I didn't.

After awhile, he said he'd have to get on back to Fullington's and start early in the morning with the horses. O, yes, those horses!

I walked with him to his horse, tied to the yard fence and that was that, except that his parting words were: "Run along in, Little-un. I think the Angels will look after girls like you."

I did and they have.

I have not seen you for many years. I am not even sure where you are, but wherever, thank you, Tony.

Mason

I think there is no one who can say exactly when Charley Mason made his first trip to the little valley on South Clear Creek, later to be known as Hermit, or whether he was alone or accompanied as he often was later, by a brother-in-law Clayton Wetherill. Certain it is that he made many trips there before he and his family were permanently established.

Originally from Wisconsin, he had come to Mancos, Colorado, where he married Anna Wetherill, and for a time took an active part in the ranching business of the B. K. Wetherills - Quaker stock from the East. He was co-discoverer and explorer with the "Wetherill Boys" of the Mesa Verde Cliff Dweller Ruins. The economic situation at the Alamo Ranch plus the fact, probably, that at heart he was no rancher and was somewhat tired and, perhaps, disillusioned as to mummies and archeology in general, influenced him to see other fields. Also, he was young and endowed amply with the spirit of the adventurer - a spirit that never left him. When quite elderly he once told me that his feeling about death was Expectancy: that it would be pleasant and interesting to live again on Mars or/and Jupiter - a sort of planet-hopping!

He had in mind getting into fish culture and this sent him looking for a suitable location for such business. He explored the country from Mancos into the San Luis Valley. His trips were, of necessity, made mostly by horseback and from Mancos by way of the Pine River and Weminuche Pass to the headwaters of the Rio Grande. I like to envision what he saw as he rounded a turn on the trail travelled by Indians and later by those intrepid and adventuresome white hunters and trappers who had come that way.

Mountain valleys so often surprise one. When the earth appears an endless chain of peaks, rocky ridges, steep slopes and forests, suddenly there it is! This little valley walled on one side by thick spruce timber and on the other by grassy slopes with large aspen groves. Through the grassy meadowlands runs willow-bordered South Clear Creek. These meadows were dotted with wild flowers, mountain flax, in particular. I have never known a spot where it was more profuse. The "flats" were blue with it!

There was already in the midst, a natural lake and Mason saw at once another could be built at a spot a short way below. Eventually this was done by means of hand scrapers and teams - a far cry from today's earth-moving machinery!

First, the land had to be acquired and this was done by various members of the family homesteading one hundred sixty acres per tract - Mason, his daughter Marion, Clayton Wetherill, Grandmother Marion Wetherill (Mason's mother-in-law), and another tract was purchased from a Fred Burrows whose homestead included the natural lake and which, by the time Mason located in the valley, was not open for homesteading. The law making it available was passed later. Altogether there were eight hundred acres in Hermit Lakes. The name "Hermit was bestowed upon the first lake built by Mason. He said the idea came to him the first summer before he brought his family from Mancos - said he felt he was living the life of a hermit!

Mason's homestead was the first homestead to be patented for the sole purpose of raising trout for market in the United States. His, also, was the first license issued for raising trout for market. This same Number 1 license was retained throughout the years the business was carried on.

A hatchery was built and 100,000 Brook trout eggs were purchased and shipped from Plymouth, Massachusetts, and hatched in this little hatchery during the winter of 1901-1902. This was the first winter Mason and his family stayed at Hermit. The little trout did so well, another lot - 200,000 - was bought. From these first Brook trout came all this variety in the Upper Rio Grande area. Mason, at first, tried stocking the Native Cut-Throat trout, but for some reason they would not stay in the lakes, so he settled with the Brook.

Later a fish hatchery was built on Spring Creek - log at first and later a stone building which still stands. This stone building was constructed by Justice Tompkins (Grandmother Wetherill's brother) assisted by Clayton Wetherill. The latter assumed the hatchery business and carried this on for many years, shipping eggs to far-away places, including Australia. Mason and his family sometimes spent the winters out, in those early years; sometimes at Del Norte and at other times nearer: the Workman Ranch (now Freemons').

Though winters were long, in one sense they were not for there was much to be done in the way of work and all had some sort of special project or hobby. Charley Mason was a self-taught taxidermist and taught the art to a daughter (Marion) who later went to work for Jack Miles and Edith at their shop in Denver.

A piano was purchased, mainly with money earned by trapping muskrats, etc., and lessons were taken by correspondence. A telephone was installed in 1910, which must have eased the isolation considerably. Incidently, the first message Marion received told of the death of her uncle, Richard Wetherill, assassinated by Indians at Mancos.

An incident before the advent of the telephone is worth recording. One winter Mason had to make a trip out on business, presumably to Creede, i.e. no farther. He traveled on skis with a stop-over, going and coming, at the Workman Ranch. However, after he reached Creede he felt the business required his going on to Denver by train. There was no way to let his family know, and when he did not return to Hermit after a lee way of two or three days, Mrs. Mason took her skis and started out down the valley. In the afternoon, two of the girls, Marion and Luella, became worried. Not having extra skis or snowshoes, they decided to improvise some from old bedsprings (net type) and light boards. With these they managed to travel over the snow (six feet deep) for a short way, but coming night and cold persuaded them to return home. Shortly after, their mother and father came in, having met several miles down the way.

They were a happy lot and most interesting, though life was rugged, to say the least. Perhaps the isolation was not felt too much - in fact, I am sure it was not, because of various trips made during the time of year when they could be away. They visited relatives in Texas and Arizona and attended the World's Fair, celebrating the opening of the Panama Canal. Also they had many interesting friends who visited them during the summer months. Some of these people I was fortunate in meeting, among them Albert Moses, a practicing attorney in Alamosa, who had been in Creede during the "boom days." He related many fascinating tales to me during his visits. Once he had a nephew, Moultrie Moses, with him, and a real honest-to-goodness Admiral, with whom I had lengthy discussions regarding the functions of the Navy. I had no hesitancy about voicing some faults I felt it had! Youth rushing in where in mature years I wouldn't!

Looking with objectivity in these later years, I think I am impressed especially with what I think was genuine pleasure these people derived from their every-day life. It is true they built up a substantial and going business -- Mr. Mason was one of the first among a very few who paid Income Tax when that "innovation was perpetrated on us! - but it was not just a way of making a living, it was a way of life itself. I so thoroughly enjoyed them all, and the accounts they gave of the place and business they had established.

A daughter said: "We traveled every route possible between Mancos and Hermit, during those early years, but most often by way of Weminuche Pass, on horseback." I can't think of a more satisfactory way. I know for I have done this. The scenery is beyond my powers to adequately describe -

towering peaks, grassy slopes, small streams, waterfalls, little nameless lakes (more fascinating because of their namelessness) that are ponds in reality but in existence even in dry seasons.

The trail winds through the most magnificent spruce timber I have ever seen, so close one's hair is brushed first on one side and then on the other. And the air one breathes so fresh, so fragrant, so exhilarating; there is no thought other than it is good to just be alive!

On one of the trips over Weminuche, Mr. and Mrs. Mason and their five little girls stopped overnight at Howard Graham's place on the Pine River. In the morning, Graham went with them up the trail to a spot where he had set a bear trap. In the trap was a huge bear and to one little girl: "the biggest, blackest, scariest" animal she had ever seen! This was their last trip over the Pass, and they did not have enough horses for all the family and the packs too, so relates Marion: "Turns were taken in walking, though Father walked most of the way, of course!" As they neared the top of the Pass, snow seemed imminent so Mason decided to go on with the packs over the Divide and then to return for the family whom he left plodding their way up the trail. A stream of sizable proportions had to be crossed, and here little Marion had difficulty forcing her way through a large willowbrush. She said it was like trying to get through the bars of a cage, and "Mother thought I wasn't trying hard enough and she and the others went on up the trail, leaving me in a screaming panic. I thought I would either have to make my way or be left behind, and this, apparently, gave me additional impetus, for I finally got through with a few scratches and bruises and caught up with them."

Before Mason returned, snow had begun to fall in earnestness, and since there was no use in getting soaked, the mother, who was wearing a very full coat, crawled under the drooping branches (they surround these big trees and touch the ground) of a large spruce, and the children huddled under her coat like a brood of chickens under a hen. Snow kept falling until it was like a blanket around them, for possibly an hour, amounting to about four inches, when "Mother saw Father coming but he did not see us as his hat was pulled low and his head bent as though following tracks. She called to him, asking what he thought he was following and he answered, 'an ol' she-bear and cubs!' Whereat Mother was furious until he explained that down the trail he had found tracks." The bear had passed close by but because of the snow, Mrs. Mason had not seen them. They all mounted their horses and went on to the Rio Grande where the snow had stopped, and home that evening.

Some years later - 1914-15? - Clayton Wetherill, his wife and their two sons, Gilbert and Carroll, made a summer field trip into the area of the dwelling places of the "Anazazi" - Cliff ruins - guiding a party of famous archeologists. These were men from the American Museum of Natural History - Dr. Prudden of Columbia University (author of "Prehistoric Ruins of the San Juan Watershed), et al. They made the trip with horses and pack-mules by way of the Weminuche and Pine. At the time, Carroll Wetherill was about four and rode back of the saddle with his mother. He recalls the steepness of the trail up Weminuche, which was on the opposite side of the stream from the present trail. In places he was quite frightened looking over cliffs and sheer rocks along and in the trail itself, and hung onto "Mama" for all he was worth! Some fifty years or so later, while elk hunting in the same area, he found himself needing to use the old trail as a short-cut, and in spite of it being dark, decided to try to locate this. It seems incredible but he did - Carroll has always had good night vision - and in going along, touched a metal sign nailed to a spruce tree: Prevent Forest Fires. It was one of the first such signs put out by the Forest Service and had the name of the then President of the United States on it, Theodore Roosevelt. The surprising thing is that the sign had weathered so well!

Another literally "hair-raising" event occurred when they were making this trip another time but by the same route. Gilbert Wetherill, a small boy, riding back of his mother, somehow fell off and into the stream - rushing white water most of its way. Amazingly and fortunately, she managed to grab him by his hair to safety! He remembers that as a result of the incident, he had frequent nightmares and his grandmother, Dr. Mary Ann Faunce, would take him into her bed to comfort and assuage. This same little grandmother was among the very early women medical doctors of America.

I cannot leave this family without particular mention of Grandmother Wetherill - Mrs. Mason's mother - whom I knew and loved dearly. She was a doughty little lady in her eighties and I suspect was sometimes something of a pain-in-the-neck to her family, though they loved her. I was not fortunate enough to know Grandfather Wetherill as he had died at Mancos several years before, but I think he and Grandmother Marion were well-matched as they say he was a peace-loving but fiery (paradox?) Quaker driven from his native Ireland because of his religious and political convictions. For a time he had acted as a Government Agent, dealing in Indian Affairs, during President Grant's administration. At that time his wife and children were living in Missouri. Grandmother Wetherill had evidently treasured his letters for she had a stack of them and on occasion would read me passages from them. I once asked her if I might take them to read, assuring her I would be ever so careful with them. The little lady said: "O, no! My dear! These letters were written by a husband to his wife and it would be unseemly for a young girl to read them!" Then I nearly DIED of curiosity! Her brother, Justice Tompkins, who at that time was a resident of Hermit with the Masons, and whom I adored as "Uncle Jut," she always addressed as "Mr. Tompkins!"

It seems appropriate at this time to relate something of the Bent family with whom I was privileged to be closely associated for many years. Herbert C. Bent's father, and grandfather to several of the Bent children in my little mountain school, was Charles Hammond Bent. He was by heritage endowed with an adventuresome spirit. His wife, Amanda Jane

Carr Bent (Jennie), was of the same. The Carrs came to Boston in 1635 and the Bents in 1638. Both families were associated with the Massachusetts Bay Company. As time passed, members of both families sought new lands and fortunes with the result that Amanda Jane Carr and Charles Hammond Bent were married in Oswego, Kansas, December 23, 1868. While living there, he held various public offices, including that of legislative representative at the Capitol in Topeka. In passing, it is interesting to note that Charles and William Bent, who built and operated Bents' Fort in southeastern Colorado (territory) in the 1830's, were cousins. I remember Bert Bent saying that there was always a "Charles Bent" in the family - his eldest son a Charles.

Mining fever apparently struck Charles Hammond Bent, as it did so many in those days, for he gathered together his family and goods in covered wagons and drove to Lake City, Colorado, in 1876, arriving shortly after a treaty had been made with the Ute Indians, whereby lands were made accessible for settlement by Whites. There Bent engaged in mining and also served in the State Legislature as representative from that area. He died in 1896, from the old ailment: Miners' Consumption, and is buried in the Lake City cemetery. A peak next to Carson Peak is named for him.

In the late 1890's, his sons Herbert C. and Ralph H. and daughter Edith M. homesteaded land (the San Juan Ranch) west of the present Wright Ranch.

About 1898, Herbert (the Bert I came to know so well) married Eva Morgan of Lake City, whom I never knew but of whom I write elsewhere. I did meet Edith Bent who married Ralph Whinnery, whose brother "Webb" was prominent in early day business in Lake City. After the death of his wife, Eva, in 1900, Bert married Deborah Mason in 1904. They lived in California for a number of years and then returned to Hermit where I met them.

Grandmother Bent (Amanda Jane), Bert's mother, came to stay with them at Hermit in 1927, and it was there in February, 1928, that she died, full of grace and years at eighty-five.

Snow was deep that winter and trips by team and sled, long and arduous, and as little travel as possible was engaged in. It was managed. A casket was brought up from Creede, thirty miles away, and with a few neighbors in attendance (ten and twelve miles distant), after a brief and very sweet service in the Bent home, the little lady was laid to rest in a grave prepared in the deep-frozen earth, mainly by a teenaged grandson.

Some may be prone to think this funeral rather barbarous. It was not. It was simple and beautiful. When spring came Grandmother's body was exhumed and taken to Lake City and interred beside her husband, Charles Hammond Bent.

Fullingtons

My association with the Fullingtons was rather brief but rewarding. Much that I know of them I learned from others.

"Rube," as he was known to all, was from all accounts, a "fixture" at the Wason ranch, famous for many years for its horses. L. S. Officer, who knew Rube then, said that as a rider and trainer of horses, he was excelled by none. He was also a sort of silent partner of Mr. Wason and many were the stories he told of his days there.

The stockyards were at Wason then. Through the years, Mr. Wason kept a sort of open house for stockmen of the area. There were meals and beds for them and stable and feed for their horses. A cook was present through the shipping seasons (in and out), sometimes a man, sometimes a woman.

"Boots" Miller (or Mueller) told me of an incident relative to this that occurred one fall. The cook at the time was a young woman, a blond, nice looking with a good figure and an abundance of almost golden hair which she wore in braids wound around her head like a coronet. One day she was in the process of mixing a batch of bread - the yeast kind. There were several of the fellows in the kitchen visiting and watching - probably waiting for the freight train, almost never on time. The girl had the bread at a soft or "sponge" stage when she leaned, reaching for some article, and one of the daring men pinched her. She said nothing, picked up the bread bowl and emptied the contents on the head of the pincher, who was, by the way, baldheaded and should have known better! What a mess! Boots concluded his story by saying that the girl helped clean it all up and good-naturedly started another batch of bread. There was no more pinching!

After Rube Fullington married Avis Mickey of Del Norte, they took up land in the North Clear Creek area and established Pearl Lakes, named for a daughter, Pearl. The property is now a Club with privately owned summer homes with several additional lakes having been built. The name Pearl Lakes seems especially appropriate as the lakes, blue and glowing in the sunshine, are like pearls on a string. I think Avis would approve.

I liked the Fullingtons - both of them - though for different reasons. He was, putting it mildly, "rough and tough," and she was, to my mind, a "lady" in the best sense of the word. Once, apropos of what, I've forgotten, I said something as to Rube's characteristics and she remarked: "Yes, but one can grow tired, sometimes, of elegance!"

Mason cabins at Hermit.

Hauling in fuel at Hermit.

Mabel Steele, Hermit, 1916.

A serious-eyed Tony, off to war.

San Juan Ranch School about 1920. Mabel Wright, teacher, at left in doorway.

Mason's home in winter, about 1912 in Hermit.

Barn at Hermit.

Hermit Barn in the building.

Charley Mason fishing at Hermit.

Bent home on San Juan Ranch. Eva Morgan Bent's grave on hillside in background.

San Juan School and teacher Mabel Wright, 1920.

My dear Second Father, Clayton Wetherill.

Wetherill home at Fish Hatchery. Mrs. Clayton Wetherill and mother, Dr. Mary Faunce on porch.

Barn at Hermit.

Grandmother Wetherill, Hermit, 1916.

Pupils -- The Bent children at Hermit.

Galloway's Stage Stop on San Juan Ranch (see Brewster).

Earl Brown in front of Barn (Molly's son).

As in 1918 Molly Brown's House and mine.

Mabel Wright's House (nee Molly Brown's) 1925.

Mr. & Mrs. Officer, 50th Wedding Anniversary.

Eva Morgan Bent's grave – San Juan Ranch.

Dollie Brooks' baby's (Hermione) grave on San Juan Ranch.

My Sister the Stove, displaced May 1, 1976.

Stoney Pass.

L. S. OFFICER

Lora S. Officer was born in Eagleville, Missouri, December 24, 1873. So soon after the Civil War, times were hard, jobs few and wages low. In 1890, at seventeen, he left home working his way to Pueblo, Colorado, where he expected to meet an older brother, Clarence. He arrived in Pueblo with just four dollars only to leam that his brother had gone to Cotopaxi. Lora got a job as a waiter in a cafe at fifty cents a day plus meals. This did not last. He said, in relating his story years later: "I must have been the clumsiest, most awkward greenhorn that ever set a cup of coffee - and that on the wrong side! - beside a diner."

Next was a job driving a team with a slip-scraper, east of Pueblo, building the Holbrook Ditch, at one dollar seventy-five cents per day. Board and room was three-fifty per week. This did not last either, and he went to work as a dishwasher in a restaurant. While at this, he would walk to the outskirts of the town to sleep under a tree to save rent. A short time later he left for Cotopaxi where he found work with D. H, Hoover Construction Co., building and widening tracks of the Rio Grande and Southern Railway. near Placerville. Here he had many wild experiences, especially so for a young man - really scarcely more than a boy - who had been reared in a home where good manners and good morals prevailed as a matter of course. There were many ill-characters of all sorts about. One night the Cockney cook went berserk with a fourteen-inch knife, in the sleep-tent. With the help of Bill Morrow (Hoover's partner), Officer managed to get the knife. This Bill Morrow was, in Officer's words: a "clean" man. This was fortunate for the boy who liked and respected him. Lora said his only vice was smoking. From this job Officer went to Telluride and from there to Del Norte. At Del Norte, the young man found work as a "Jerk-line" driver with a freight outfit. This involved skill of a sort and certainly difficult for an inexperienced man. That Officer mastered this speaks well of his ability to learn quickly. I know nothing of this sort of driving, first hand, and can only repeat what was told to me by various people who managed it. It involved six to eight horses or mules. The driver, or "skinner", rode the left wheel mule and drove with a jerk-line. This line or rein ran to the outer side of the bridle of the left leader, whose head was connected with the right lead animal by a light pole. The mules were trained to turn right in response to repeated short jerks on the reins and turn left by steady pulling on the line. Mules were used generally in mountain freighting.

Officer had arrived in Del Norte shortly after Thanksgiving Day, 1890. After about three weeks he went home to Missouri for a visit, having saved enough money for the trip. In March, 1891, he returned to Pueblo, as he said: richer in experience than in cash, although in better financial state than when he had arrived the year before.

For a time he worked in a fourteen-arch brick kiln - this was very hard work - where he met a Jack Kirby (an alias, as he was a U.S. Army deserter) who drank heavily, but, along with other fatherly admonitions, advised the younger man against liquor.

Lora Officer came to Creede for the first time February 11, 1892, at the height of the Boom. A population of 15,000 was claimed but probably there were less than 12,000 people. So much has been written of Creede's early days that there is little point in going into this. In fact, Officer, in telling his story, dwelt only briefly on those days, saying only that there was not much law and a lot of riotous activity.

He found employment with Dan Hoover and Bill Morrow, the same contractors on the D. & R. G. Railway. project at Placerville. They now had a transportation business at Creede, with ore-wagons, transfer, express-wagons, livery vehicles, along with a livery-bam, pack-trains (mule and burro), and they employed thirty-five to fifty men. Because of the need for suitable meals for them, they set up a boarding-house. It was a tent, eighty feet long, twenty feet wide, with boarded-up sides and a dirt floor - railroad style - with a kitchen at one end. There were rows of benches and tables. There was a cook with two helpers known as "flunkies," one of whom was Officer. Food was served "family Style": ample, simple and good. Many other than Hoover-Morrow employees ate there. This boarding-house stood where the Elk's building now stands.

As before stated, I do not wish to repeat what has already been written of the early history of Creede, but I do feel I should try to give something of Lora Officer's impressions and views of the times. He knew Soapy Smith: about the Petrified Man, etc. In fact, Bill Perry, Hoover's Express-wagon driver, came into breakfast excited over his night's experience. He had helped excavate and bring in the petrified man from Dry Gulch and he was sure it was really a petrified human body. It was placed on a slab in a tent about ten feet northeast of Hoover's place and a charge of twenty-five cents made for viewing. Officer was among the gullible ones, of course! An attempt was made to steal the figure and in this an arm was broken off and taken to the Theatre Comique - a "Leg Show," Officer said. It was later returned.

Upon hearing that Bob Ford had been shot, Officer ran to Ford's tent and, peering through a crack, saw the body lying on the floor. He said that, at the time, many people were in sympathy with the killer, Ed O'Kelly.

For sometime Officer had been buying supplies for the boarding-house so had gained experience which persuaded him to become a partner of Barney Gaughran in a Meat and Grocery Market. Officer did most of the delivery business with a buck-board up West Willow to Bachelor, down to Weaver, Creede and Jimtown - six days a week. He was nineteen years old now. A crony of his - an employee of that aforementioned "Theatre Comique" - and he had batching quarters at the rear of the store. One evening he gleefully exhibited three fryers (chickens) - said he had found them wandering in the street: "Pore lil' orphans!" Officer said they should cook them for supper and the two proceeded to dress them on the spot, openly. The

James Henry family lived just acoss the way and were the owners of the fowl. It so happened that several of the daughters -- one of these girls, Ina Henry, later became Officers wife. She never ceased, at times, through the years, to tease by saying that she had married a common chicken thief!

In 1894, Officer sold his interest in the market to Gaughran for $200.00, and with his older brother, Clarence, went to the mining camp of Dubois in the Gunnison area. They did not stay long as mining "petered out," and Officer returned to Creede - Clarence went to Pueblo - the town and/or area he would never quit. He went to work for C. E. Emery, Groceries and Meats.

On February 17th, 1895, he married Ina Florence Henry, in the Henry home which stood about sixty yards from what had been Bob Ford's saloon. The Rev. Foster performed the ceremony.

In his work with the butcher in the Emery market, Officer learned how to judge and buy beef "on the hoof' and to cut up meat expertly. Shortly, he and Charley Maag (the butcher) established their own shop at the lower end of town. Their equipment consisted mainly of a meat-block, some saws and knives.

Officer did the buying for the meat market. At first he was able to buy cattle on foot in small lots from local ranchers, among them Dan Soward of the Soward ranches farther up the Rio Grande. Later he had to go farther afield and went into the Cebolla valley area. He told of getting twenty head of hay- fed steers at forty dollars per head from the Ernest Foster ranch (now the Howard place) and driving them, ten at a time, to Creede where they were butchered.

Officer always credited Maag with teaching him to become the expert meat-cutter he was. The two could "dress" a beef in thirty minutes. Officer taught a daughter (May) to cut meat and this she could do adeptly with help in handling the carcass.

Anent the Maags: they seem to have led a stormy sort of life. She drank and on one occasion took a shot (gun, I mean) at him as he rode up to the shop, but, fortunately, he was aware of her in time to lie low on his horse so she missed him. Charley Streams, the marshal, arrested her but this did not deter the lady once she was free. She continued her harassing which included throwing a rock through the big plate-glass window of the store and pouring kerosene into a barrel of pickles. The couple was finally divorced and both left town, though not together! Officer then opened a meat-grocery with Fred Burrows as a partner. This same Fred Burrows had owned the upper Hermit lake which he sold to Charley Mason for $3,000.00, a good price for those times. Officer continued to do the meat buying. On some of his trips to the Cebolla country, he was accompanied by a young friend, Lester Mumford - step-son of George Snyder. They had many hectic experiences, e.g. a wild steer startled by a chattering chipmunk would send the whole bunch into willow-groves from which they were hard to dislodge. However, as cattle people know, if the stock are allowed to proceed slowly, usually they give no great trouble.

About this time, Officer and Bill Bader filed homestead claims of 150 acres each, in Blue Creek Park and went into the cattle business together. They bought the cattle from George Martin. It was a bad year - no hay to be had - and straw was six dollars per ton. They ran the cattle in chico brush country northeast of Monte Vista. Needless to say, they lost money. Meanwhile, they worked on their homesteads, building fences, corrals etc. Officer's father being ill in St Louis, he made a trip to see him, and upon returning, stopped to see about the cattle. He found them so poor he decided, then and there, to have no more until he had a ranch of his own upon which to run them.

He found just a place, the San Juan ranch, of 480 acres, twenty-one miles west of Creede, priced at $3500.00. He and Bader dissolved partnership and divided the cattle. Officer moved his to his new ranch. All the while he had continued with the meat-market business in Creede, but he now sold this to his brother, Clarence, and Dr. Samuel MeKibbin, and moved to the ranch. This was June, 1905.

Officer then filed on an adjoining 160 acres which made him a ranch of 640 acres. A very good piece of meadow land was included in this and grew much hay - more than he needed for his stock so that he baled and sold the surplus.

At this time he had been married ten years and had five children. A residence was maintained in Creede for several years or until a school was established (two schools, really; one at the Officer ranch for the winter term; the other at Hermit for the summer), so Mrs. Officer and the children came to the ranch for summers only.

These were busy years and happy years. There were no cars, and roads at times made poor traveling for wagons and teams and even for horsetrips to Creede. There were few so-called "tourists" - a few coming to the Texas Club, later known as the Workman ranch. Fishing was fantastic in the Rio Grande and smaller streams, and there were no restrictions. Officer liked to fish and was an especially good fly-fisherman.

Neighbors were "NEIGHBORS" in a strict sense of the word. There were no telephones but word always got around when anyone planned a trip to town and when road conditions were bad the neighbors gathered to help build culverts etc. Also, no one made a trip to Creede without stopping at each place as he went along, to take mail in and ascertain if any errands needed doing or supplies to be brought out. There was time for visiting, too. I remember Officer telling me that often when he stopped at Browns' (the Wright ranch now), Mrs. Brown (Molly) would say: "O, Lora, don't go on today. Stay and we'll play cards and you go on tomorrow." This he did if he was not in a rush; otherwise, he went on and stopped over night when he returned. Years later he said this: "Mabel, in those days when we had to get around with wagons or horse-back, we always had time to visit with our neighbors. Now we have cars and trucks that 'whiz' us on our way but we are lucky if we see each other two or three times a year!" Of course, this was after

Officers and others began to "go out" for the winters –he had sold his cattle and gone into the sheep business, wintering them at a place near Del Norte which he had purchased.

During those early years, there were many incidents of which I learned in talking to Lora Officer. He described in detail a trip he made from Silverton over Stony Pass. He said he was quite sure he was the last to make the trip with a team and wagon. He and Mel Garde had been to Aztec, New Mexico, and decided to come back via Stony. It was not smooth going at best, but they had real trouble when they encountered a rockslide which had centered the road and no feasible way around it. They unhitched the team, uncoupled the wagon and dragged the two parts by hand over and around the rocks!

In addition to selling extra hay, Officer further supplemented his income by freighting supplies (e.g. cement) to the Rio Grande reservoir, then known as the Farmers' Union, during its construction. He operated a sawmill above the ranch and also did some work for the Forest Service.

These were good years for him and his family. In a sense, all years were good. He was basically a happy man and though he had his share of human troubles, illnesses and sorrow - losing all three of his sons must have been a terrific blow - he and his Ina were, somehow, able to take these things with dignified acceptance.

Lora Officer was not a worrier. He said that as a young man, he had resolved never to let worry over petty matters keep him from enjoying a good nights rest at the day's end. I am sure he kept his resolution as far as was possible. He was a good husband, a good father - there were ten children who grew to adulthood, all bom in Creede and all but one in the same house! – and certainly a good neighbor.

He was fond of young people. He had a great sense of humor and was quite witty - often joking and "kidding" with Mrs. Officer and the children. He laughed a lot. He loved the ranch and the work he did there.

Not long before he died, I stopped at the Officer home in Del Norte, en route home from a trip to Alamosa. It was early evening, in late fall I think, and lights were on. Mrs. Officer and three of the daughters welcomed me as a long absent member of the family, and, indeed, I felt myself so. After a short visit, they insisted I "Go see Papa" who had gone to bed but they were sure was not yet asleep.

I went to his room and found him propped up on his pillows with a bedlight on. I sat down beside him and at once started teasing him, saying something like: this is a fine thing! It's only six o'clock and I can remember the time when you would not be caught in bed so early! He laughed and said: "Well, Mabel, I have had my supper - and a good supper it was - and my bed feels good to my old bones. I have been lying here thinking of all the waters that have gone under the bridge since I took up the Ranch."

Brewster

In writing of these "Early Ones," I must not omit Lorenzo Dow Brewster, known as "L. D." or "Ren" to his familiars.

He came with his father to Silverton in the early seventies. They were interested in mining but after a short time decided to devote their time and attention to another business associated with the mining industry: that of getting supplies to the mining camps of the area and particularly to Silverton, by means of stage lines from Del Norte on up the Rio Grande. Mainly, Brewsters operated by freighting goods from the stage-stop at Galloway's (now the San Juan Ranch) which was designated a "break-bulk" station, to Silverton by way of rugged Stony Pass. For the most part this was done with mules, horses, and sometimes on skis or snowshoes in winter. Wagons were used for the route at certain seasons though the going was rough.

Brewsters had a cabin for living quarters and a stable above the now existent Rio Grande Reservoir. All signs of these are gone but "Brewsters' Park" still designates the spot. There was a sort of sub-station on Grassy Hill maintained by a Squire Watson. Also, "Broncho Dan Galloway" had a cabin near the mouth of Weminuche Creek. But, on the whole, it was a lonely area, inhabitance-wise.

There were nine in the Brewster family: the father and mother, five sons and two daughters. I doubt that they were all together at Brewsters' Park at any time. The family home was in Baxter Springs, Kansas. Ren was the son who was with his father during those freighting days. At this time he was seventeen, a slender, husky youngster, well-equipped for the rugged life.

It was a rugged life, indeed, this freighting business. In fact, I would feel that it was so hard that L. D. Brewster could never have retained any fond memories of his experiences, were it not for a few references he made during our association. Added to this, was his regular return to the Upper-Rio Grande country, years later.

I first saw him, an erect, broad-shouldered six-footer standing in the gateway to our ranch barnyard, gazing intently across our meadows to the mountains beyond. There was something arresting in his very posture. He wore a black suit and a large western-style black hat. He was not young, one sensed, despite his carriage - he was past eighty - so when he called to me, rather bruskly: "Come here!" I went to him. He began questioning me about the roads and trails leading up country, starting with a statement that the road, "such as it was" had gone below that barn across Crooked Creek through the meadows. I answered as best I could, concluding with the remark that he must have been in this area a long time ago. "Sixty years," he replied, and then, turning to me, "Say, Girl, can't we get something to eat?" He had two friends with him, a lady who was the daughter of a former business partner of his, and her son, a young man of perhaps twenty-five or so.

Though contrary to our practice of no service meals to transients - we were cattle ranchers - (some good fairy must have prompted me) I assured him that they certainly could be fed, and lead them into the ranch-house and shortly to the table. After eating, L. D. Brewster took out the biggest, blackest cigar I ever saw and proceeded to smoke it while drinking a second cup of coffee. I think the coffee did itl The Wright men liked their coffee black and strong enough to leap from the pot into the cup when whistled for, and so it seemed did Brewster. He then asked about accommodations for the three of them. They stayed six weeks and came to us regularly through the summers for many years - until the last year of his life.

I have given him this introduction as a sort of portrait of the man who gave me such a graphic picture of our country and life as it was in the seventies and early eighties. In so doing, he brought much of interest and richness into my life.

I will touch on only a few of the incidents he described. As I inferred in the beginning, the hardships endured, while he and his father and sometimes a brother or two operated their business, might have soured L. D. on the whole country. That was untrue, I feel assured from various stories he told me of those days. He once said that the reason for his coming back after those sixty years was to get acquainted with the new generation, sit on the front porch and watch the crazy Texans go by. He never did much traveling about the country, refusing point blank to go farther up the River than the Rio Grande Reservoir, though there was some travel as far as Beartown by light trucks - these being pre-jeep days.

I am sure few people can appreciate how much depended on the skill of a man who operated a pack train in those days. The loads on the burros and mules had to be properly balanced, as an insecure load could throw the animal off balance and over a cliff. Most of the time the mules or burros were tied together in tandem for if one slipped the linkage could save it. Also, I have been told that mules were led and burros driven.

One particularly hard winter Brewster had the job of taking a horse from Silverton to the Highland Mary mine. If you have been in this area, you know the situation of the mine. I can liken it only to Shangri La. That snowy and, worse, icy, trail must have made the young man quail at times. He had snowshoes but what about the horse? Well, L. D. put its feet into sacks partially filled with shavings and excelsior left from packing cases. The sacks were of tightly-woven cotton and known as "seamless," and I doubt the West would have been won without them as they were put to many uses - from storing food away from flies to kitchen roll-towels. These he tied securely around the horse's legs and they went on to the Highland Mary.

He said that of all the goods that the freighter found the "meanest" to pack, it was soda crackers in barrels. They were unwieldly and they could get wet if snow was falling and "It always was," he added.

On one occasion, he was delayed because of having waited for payments due him, thus missing, narrowly, a snowslide that caught three men. One of them had a glass-eye and L. D. had the job of taking the corpse to Del Norte for shipment East. The body was placed in a crude sort of box with slats across the top and put on a toboggan which he, on snowshoes, pulled over Stony Pass and on to Galloway's. He said it was the spookiest trip he ever made, as any time he looked back that eye seemed to wink at him!

One afternoon when I happened to be alone shelling peas on the south porch of the kitchen, Mr. Brewster took a chair nearby. The talk was desultory -- certainly on my part, for I knew better than to demand a story from him. He talked when and if he liked and held strictly to his own mind and ideas. Finally, I said something about the scarcity of people in the area and along the trails he knew in those old days, and he proceeded to tell me the following story:

He was riding alone minus a pack-train from Silverton, home to Brewster Park. It was in late summer and the only humans he'd seen had been a small group of Indian squaws (Utes) picking berries. I don't know just where this was but I am told that it was customary for many Silverton miners' families to go miles up in the Pass area to gather elderberries, raspberries and other wild berry fruit. Anyway, the young man, stopping to water his horse at a spring, heard a child crying, and caught a glimpse of something in the willows. It was a little Indian girl, eleven or twelve years old. She had caught her ankle between some rocks bruising and cutting it considerably, and had come to the spring to bathe it. L. D. said she was a pretty, little dark-eyed thing and almost as shy as a deer. He managed to coax her to let him help her. He had an ointment of some sort in his saddle-bags, and after applying this and bandaging the ankle with a handkerchief, he put her up on his horse and took her back to the camp where he set her down and rode away. He looked back once and saw her standing as he had left her. He raised a hand in farewell and she raised hers in answer. He finished the story, was silent a few minutes looking up-river and said: "She had pretty eyes. Ah, well!" and rising, stalked off to harass the Texans.

Mr. Brewster had decided notions as to how his food was prepared and I soon learned I must take responsibility for this. He liked his bacon cooked very lightly, just to the clear stage, and his coffee - well, I have already mentioned that! He was very fond of beans seasoned with bacon fat and lots of pepper and when we had them, he never failed to demand vinegar for them. This I never had, having been warned by his family that it would make him ill. When I regretted the lack of vinegar, he would remark: "So! Next time I go into Creede I'll get you a whole barrel of vinegar!" What a fine man he was!

INTERLUDE

I enjoy walks or small hikes in the vicinity of my home. These must, of necessity, be generally in the fall of the year, after the busy summer is over. One of my favorites is a walk across our pastures and big meadow into those of the San Juan ranch.

In a southwestern corner there is a great mound of eons-old rock and earth. Geologically, it is glacial drift left behind when the sun won over that great tool of ice that gouged, scratched and shaped this Upper-Rio Grande area.

I climb up over the crumbly rock and large boulders and through wild-currant bushes whose tenacity has taken root for them. At the top is another mound - a tiny one but not to be over-looked or missed. It is a caim of rocks and it marks the grave of one Dollie Brooks' baby girl who came into the world and out about 1888. The group of neighbors who assisted with the interment gathered rocks near at hand and covered the little heap of earth, placing a larger one at the head and so left it.

Hearing of this episode, others have sought out the grave and somehow it came about that each visitor carried a stone and added it to the original marker. I always bring either a pretty rock I have picked up along the river as I walked along, or a mineral specimen from one of Creede's mines.

This day in the fall of 1976, I have a piece of amethyst quartz and I place this among the mottled stones of the cairn. One n tell the old ones as lichen has covered them.

I sat a long while in the warm sunshine looking over the soft gray-brown of the meadows, trying to envisage them 'way back on the days when, as one oldtimer told me, there were freighters with ox carts stretching nearly two miles from the old Texas Club place, across the Wright Ranch meadows to the stagestop at Galloway's!

Then my eyes turn to the surrounding hills, "rock-ribbed and ancient as the sun." Old Bristol Head, named for that Bristol Head in England, towers in the East, dark, inscrutible and blue. The sun neared its setting and the shadow- fingers of the hills began to teach across the valley and I came away.

O, yes! I forgot to tell the Baby's name: Hermione. Very unusual and very pretty.

She was young and she was pretty. Her hair was brown and also her eyes. Jim Workman told me her eyes reminded him of the eyes of a doe-deer. She was of medium height and slender with a graceful carriage and manner. Her father, in the short talk we had of her, said that once as a small child out walking with him in the mountain pasture, he noticed her rather cautious and light step and upon comment, she said she could not bear to crush the "sweet little bluebells." Albeit there was a sturdiness about her, and she had capable hands.

She came as a bride from the busy mining town of Lake City about the turn of the century (1898) to live with her young husband on a ranch in the Upper-Rio Grande country. The place was near the mouth of Crooked Creek Canyon and known then as now: the San Juan Ranch. Earlier there was a stage-stop here on the Del Norte-Silverton road. There were several log buildings on the place including the original inn for the stage-line. Nearby in a log-cabin not far from the box canyon of the river, the young couple began their life together. With them resided his parents, a brother and sister. It was a typical ranch with meadows that produced hay for the winter feeding of cattle summer grazed on the grassy hills above. There was irrigating, fences to keep in repair and all the various jobs that make up ranching.

It should be remembers that a ranch such as this was something to be literally carved out of the native soil with and by real brawn through long days of labor. There was little in the way of machinery. Many an irrigation ditch was dug by hand with pick and shovel. Of course, back of it all was the dream. One must marvel at the dreams of these early settlers and more at their courage and endurance. The traces of irrigation ditches intended for bringing water from Spring Creek and South Clear Creek may still be seen along the ridge north. That the project was never finished to the point of use detracts nothing from the aspiration and endeavor of the family. They were fine people with the intellect, culture and generosity to make them agreeable and interesting to others. I think they were, perhaps, rather reticent which is a far thing from indifference. They were of strong religious conviction and though they were pleased to discuss such matters seriously, they definitely did not attempt to impose their creed upon others.

The young couple was treated with kindness and special understanding and something of freedom from work routine those first several months. He was urged to take his young wife with him in excursions about the country in general: "Show her Box Canyon; Clear Creek Falls; the Squaw Creeks; Weminuchee; Lost Trail" etc. Nearby rambles they did on foot and further travel by horse-back and many were the rides they had, up in the beautiful mountain country through the summer days.

Evenings were spent with the family, reading and discussing books and the few magazines or gathering about the small organ singing old favorites. I have one of their song-books with special markings.

It was far from being all play, however, and the youthful bride shared in the simple but necessary house-hold chores. Early, she demonstrated her ability to bake excellent bread and soon this became her regular task. In late summer and early fall there was berry-picking and while the preserving and jelly-making went on, the men were out harvesting the hay-crop. Then there were trips by buckboard to Creede for staple groceries, clothing and other supplies for the coming winter. How carefully these lists had to be made! If a broom was needed but forgotten, the old one had to do!

One of the biggest jobs was getting in a supply of wood for the winter. Quantities were required for the cold months ahead. Cattle were gathered from the hills and put into the meadows now dotted with fenced-haystacks. Anent the latter, no fences could keep out marauding elk sometimes driven by deep snows down from the hills, and, on occasion, members of the family took turns in sleeping in the hay!

One of those early day housewives told me that if ever she grew tired of cooking it was in the winter for it always seemed that was ALL she did! She said everybody, especially the men, ate constantly. Whenever the door opened for a man bearing an armful of wood, there needed to be a crockfull of doughnuts or cookies at hand.

On an early spring afternoon in 1900, Bert Hosselkus stopped at the Workman place to tell Mrs. Workman that there was trouble at Bents' - baby was due and the young mother-to-be, Eva Bent, was very ill. Hosselkus was on his way with team and light wagon to Creede for a doctor. Mrs. Workman went immediately, of course, to the Bent home. She said, in telling me about the affair: "I did what I could but it was very little." Eva and her baby died and their grave can be seen in a grove of spruce and juniper on a low hill on the south side of the San Juan Ranch. When I first saw it in 1918, there was a log fence enclosure and the marker of red spruce with name and date of birth and death and a bit of scripture: "Blessed are they that sleep in the Lord," hand-carved and quite legible. There is one other grave here, that of Grace Bridgeman, a cousin of Bert Bent's.

MRS. JAMES WORKMAN

She was born Clara Gustafson in Sweden and at the turn of the century came with a sister and a brother to Denver, Colorado. They were young people and it speaks well for their courage and pioneer spirit that they would leave their native country to come to the new at that time.

Clara, probably about seventeen, appeared at Wagon Wheel Gap where she helped the McClellands operate a rooming-boarding house or hotel. Somewhere, somehow she met and married Jim Wing, owner of the old Texas Club property, a stop-over place on Clear Creek about seventeen miles out of Creede beside the highway leading to Lake City. To her, here, was born a daughter, Esther, and a son, Carl. A few months before Carl's birth Wing was no more. Various stories have been told as to his demise but a newspaper clipping states that his body was found in an alley in Pueblo and that he had been shot. Anyway, he died and Clara Wing had problems, what with a baby coming, no one to get in the winter's supply of fuel, see to the livestock (cattle) etc. Then appeared Jim Workman who had come into the neighborhood a few years previously. He was a miner, prospector, fur trapper and had homesteaded a tract of land which is now a part of Wrights' Lower Ranch. After Carl's birth, Jim Workman and Mrs. Wing married and for many years operated the Workman Ranch, nee Texas Club, now the Freemon place.

They had two sons, Emmett and Tom. Little four-year old Emmett drowned in the spring of 1912 when he was attempting to get some pussy-willows along Clear Creek beside the ranch house. His father and Arthur Wright found his body two weeks later. It had washed up onto a sand bar of the Rio Grande in the Sylvestor meadows - now a part of Wrights Ranch.

All this I learned when I came into the Wright family in 1918. Mrs. Workman was very reticent about her early personal life but this did not matter to me. I knew and loved her as a good neighbor and friend.

She was one of the most hospitable persons I ever knew. You were always welcome at her house and her table. As a cook she couldn't be excelled and we three Wrights were often guests not only at special times like Thanksgiving, etc., but often evenings for card games. Both she and Mr. Workman enjoyed cards and many were the evenings of this either at their home or ours. Not being a card- player (too stupid!) I would pop com, make candy and if she was present, play with Mrs. Workman's little granddaughter, Clara Nance.

But I think my association with Mrs. Workman holds a special place in treasured memories because of her quiet, unassuming friendliness toward me. She was always ready to help me with my housekeeping problems and I had many in those days. She was always sympathetic and most understanding. There was a sort of gaiety about her, too, and many were the times I would run down the road just to visit with her. She was always busy but always had time for me. She seldom spoke of any problem or trouble of her own though I know she had them. Particularly, never did she mention little Emmett's death though I know what a constant grief it must have been to live all those years so close to the scene. This was especially so when in later years she was rearing SEVEN grandchildren whose parents had died or otherwise left them in her care. I remember one afternoon when all seven were running around playing on the creek-side of the house. Mrs. Workman called to them, saying: "Play on the OTHER side of the house and Grandmother will make you some cookies right away!"

When aroused, I am told she would lapse into her Swedish tongue. One such incident occurred when an irrigation officer (water commissioner) attempted to shut off a small ditch carrying water to her chicken-pen! Evidently, he received a castigation in Swedish that he never forgot!

In an enclosure with several members of her family, in the Creede cemetery you can find Mrs. Workman's grave. There is a granite memorial with her name engraved on it but her true memorial lies in the hearts of those seven grandchildren and the friends who remember her.

THE HOUSE I LIVE IN

The house I live in is not mine alone. I have shared it for nearly sixty years with the original owner, Molly Brown (Mrs. Jim Brown) who came here with her husband and son, Earl, in about 1900 from Ouray, Colorado. On this ranch, made up of several homesteads, they built first - naturally! - a big red barn and then this house, a nine roomed frame structure, painted white with green trim.

However, it is mainly of the lady who reigned in it until her death in 1909, I would speak. I never met her in person but I came to "know" her nevertheless, through a close friend of the Browns who spent much time here during those years. This man, a Kentuckian, James Harbison, known familiarly as "Bear Jim" - he was a hunter and trapper - was often in my own home during my growing up years at Lake City. He held Molly Brown in the greatest esteem and, as he put it, "pleasured" in talking of her.

She was, indeed, a remarkable woman. As an infant in her cradle in Minnesota, her hands were frost-bitten and as a result she lost the tips of her fingers down to the second joint on her left hand and one finger to the first on her right hand. In spite of this handicap, she became adept at myriad accomplishments. She sewed, mostly by machine, of course, but she did mending by hand – Bear Jim said she did a fine job of mending the gloves and mittens of the men in her household.

There was one of her hand-quilted quilts here when I came. She milked, took a man's part in fence-building, irrigating, cattle-feeding and many other outside chores. She was an excellent cook and housekeeper in general. She liked to play card games and when neighbors came to spend evenings or nights she always took a hand in them. L. S. Officer of the San Juan ranch above, told me she loved to laugh, though hers was a hard life at times, almost unbearably so. In spite of it all she was a sociable person.

The building and furnishing of the ranch-house, probably brought the greatest joy she ever knew. A neighbor, Mrs. Workman, told me about this. She and Molly were good friends and each phase of the building process, the kinds of furniture, etc., were discussed. There was carpet on the three bedroom and parlor floors, green shades and white lace curtains at the windows. There was a set of gold brocade furniture in the parlor. Molly was very proud of it all. I am sure it represented and satisfied a love of beauty in contrast to other features of her life. Mrs. Workman said the crowning tough was a picture that Molly had an itinerant artist paint of the house, adding a lovely green lawn and rose bushes laden with bloom! I don't know what became of the picture.

There is not much left of the original furnishings nor was there when I took over. There is one chair of the parlor furniture. By the way, the parlor (now a bedroom) still has the original carpet. They must have made uncommonly good carpet in those days! There are two lovely old-fashioned dressers, a very solid platform rocker and a beautiful side-board of cherry wood. Some of the door hardware is lovely and there is a doorbell that everyone takes delight in ringing. There is oilcloth that Molly put on the shelves of the little closet off the living-room. It is still intact and remarkably pliable after all these years. They just don't make oilcloth like this nowadays!

When I came knowing so much about Molly Brown and so little about house keeping and learning by trial and error, I, often, when alone fancied her presence and guiding hand. Sometimes I sensed her disapproval at "what you are doing to my house!" I remember once when ironing and singing what I am sure Molly would have thought a naughty song, suddenly there was a big, clattering noise that sent me rushing outside and which later I decided was due to falling bricks in the old chimney. This often occurs in old chimneys, but I took as a reprimand from Molly and changed my time. Sometimes, however I felt her approval like a pat on the shoulder.

The house stands firm on its foundations: no sagging of doors or warped floors and window frames. Much of the roof has its original shingles and any leaks we may have, come mostly from recent additions of porches, etc. We have had stucco put on and Molly would approve as this has made the house much warmer. It needs painting again and we'll get this done one of these days. In the windows of the front porch I keep red and pink geraniums so that he who runs may read that we love our home.

MY SISTER THE STOVE

You were retired this day, May Day, 1976, after 75 years of almost constant service, some of it night duty, far beyond the call of, and I feel a compulsion to comment on our relationship from the autumn of 1918.

It was then I was formally introduced to You. You presented what I thought, a formidable appearance. Ray and I had moved from the Honeymoon cabin where we'd spent our first summer to the Big House where I was to endeavor to cook for him and his brother who would be feeding the cattle that winter and for many more to come.

It wasn't that I did not belong to Your era for I did - I was eighteen too! Also I knew how to build a fire in a wood stove and had mastered by the patience of my dear, long-suffering husband, the rudiments of some simple cooking. Poor Ray! How could any bride be as ignorant as I! I did not know "sic'em" from "come-here" about ANYTHING! But, I am not stupid and, as I said, had learned a little. However, the stove in our cabin was a very small one and uncomplicated and YOU were something else!

Ray, again, patiently instructed me as to Your draft manipulations; Your possible reactions at what I might do wrong and offend you. It was made plain that I would be the offender!

On the whole You were cooperative and I did not make too many mistakes. Most of them merely made You angry and so hot You burned my biscuits! We had seven winters in which to become acquainted and then I really took You over in 1925 when Ray and his brothers bought the Ranch from Father Wright and I moved into the ranch house to stay.

From 1925 until 1942 we served meals to our summer guests, sometimes as many as thirty, three times a day. I cooked these - rather You did - and they were big meals, all of them and the guests fell over each other to get into the diningroom.

Then, too, there were the hay-hands, often twenty or more men and teen-age boys. They ate in the kitchen and would they EAT! The big table would be turned catticorner and a smaller one put at one end. I think I enjoyed cooking for the hay crew most of all. YOU seemed to know how I felt, even at four in the morning, and seldom was there any trouble between us.

The cooking was not the only contribution You made to the welfare of mankind: I am thinking of the countless cowboys whose wet, cold boots and feet were warmed and dried as they sat with long legs poked into Your warm, open oven; the gloves and mittens a-top Your overhead warming oven; the coats hung on the water-tank that YOU kept hot; the convenience of Your reservoir on one side, the water always hot. Especially, there was the cheery crackle from You big firebox and the hum of the tea-kettle.

I looked at You this morning as You were moved through the kitchen door to the side porch. You show signs of use, many battle scars, many of which I put there. I did not cause them all, for after all, You'd been in use several years before my advent.

I see the result of the time I carelessly left You and let a kettle of grape jelly in the making, boil over Your top and down Your front onto the nice, shiny nickel.

Try as I did through the years, I was never able to erase this. You were really "burnt" over this; anyway the jelly was.

You had scarcely been installed in the new house at the turn of the century, the justified pride of Mollie Brown, when her new daughter-in-law accidently dropped the lid of the reservoir and broke one of the hinges. I'd give a pretty penny to know what Molly said about this! One had to use care is raising the lid after this, else it would fall into the tank of hot water. I had been in charge less than a week when Ray repaired the broken hinge. The mend scarcely shows so perhaps this is not really a scar. You are as efficient as ever. There is nothing wrong with You or me except that we don't belong to this era.

You never asked much of us, just fuel and a new set of fire-box grates now and then through the years. In spite of all the messes and mishaps, I think You are beautiful! It seems to me You should have at this time or retirement, some token of appreciation but What? Not a Watch, certainly, I have watched You too many years!

Perhaps, the best I can do is wish that Your new owner, who will value You probably as an "antique," a representative of the "GOOD OLD DAYS," will treat You kindly, more so than I have. I love You, STOVE.

High in the Upper Rio Grande country, there is a little Lost Ganyon - lost because it seems to have no connection with other canyons and gorges in that rugged area.

Your first thought is wonder that it could be: a perfect jewel of a Box canyon. Down, far down from the rocky walls that surround, is a tiny green glade and sure to be a small stream and a spring creating it. Your second though is how to get down there. The cliffs about, on one of which you stand, are not only steep but rough. Until over half way to the bottom they look sheer rock without bushes or small tree growth for handholds. Yet down you must go. It seems that so very green little valley is calling: "Come see!"

The going was rough indeed, and one needed the proclivities of a mountain goat to negotiate it. In fact, it seemed so much of an ordeal that you felt inclined to give up and go back but that, too, seemed as frightening as to go on. After getting around the overhanging cliff, a way appeared possible by means of a few "scraggly" trees - how I dislike to use that term for these intrepid and courageous ones - and bushes. By dint of strength of arm and absolute disregard of what happened to clothing and hide, slipping and sliding - the latter about doing for trouser seat - you are down and among spruce.

You pause for a bit of breath-taking and gaze about. It is a small meadow in this pocket in the hills. You start walking slowly, all the while struck by the profusion of wildflowers, and come to a tiny stream, large enough, however, to gurgle from one little pool to another between green turfy banks. An odd thing about this is that it transversed the little glen, not flowing lengthwise as is usual, but crosswise - a veritable paradox valley. Flowers were everywhere. The grass dotted wtih Harebell, Wild Geranium, Phlox, Pink Plumes; even Mertensia which we know as Chiming Bells. Close to the water were those precious little Elephant Heads, and water-loving Mountain Laurel and Shooting Star.

I wish you could have seen all this. I wish I might have. I did not but a friend of mine, a most estimable man, did. He knew mountain flowers better than anyone else I've ever known and he always had an eye out for new and rare ones. He told me that on this occasion he found in the crevice of rock at the foot of ascent from the canyon (he did get out!) Alpine Columbine, that lovely lavender-blue cup 'n' saucer flower that grows only in real high country and which I have seen but once in all my ramblings.

The man was spending a few days of a short vacation "prospecting 'round" - his terms - in that country above the Rio Grande Reservoir. The air was soft and warm - it was early July - and the sky above that deep blue as seen from far down in a canyon. Did you ever think that it could have been, say a sort of muggy yellow-bile green or some such? I am sure the Creator knew we needed beauty in our lives along with the necessities of air, food, water, shelter. There are explanations scientific or the like for many forces and laws of Nature. The wind, for instance, is the result of certain conditions, but what about the sounds it makes in the trees! And Color! Above all, our ability to appreciate these, to me, Extras. Our inborn sensitivity to beauty.

To resume, the man sat down on the bank of the stream to rest and muse. At first there was stillness, but after a bit came stirrings. Birds, tiny wren-like; a pine squirrel; more birds, including a Canada Jay. Birds! How full of purpose their lives even though they seem so free. Butterflies of all hues began flitting about among the flowers. How evanescent their lives yet how patently worthwhile - caterpillar, cocoon, butterfly! You just have to believe in miracles.

Time passed - an hour? In such a place, time is not. Noticing the small moundlike piles of earth, no doubt pushed up by those little moles or gophers so prevalent in the mountains, the man began idly picking with his piton hammer such as prospectors use and which he carried by a strap fastened to his belt. Surprisingly, he turned up a piece of metal, an old iron ring so crusted with rust it was a wonder it did not disintegrate as he touched it. Looking more carefully, he found another piece which was still attached to a bit of leather, so old, weathered and stiff, it fell from his hand.

Excitedly but carefully, filled with wonder, he searched. He turned up a mule shoe and what might have been a spur rowel and that was all. He said he felt he could have gone on looking for days or even months but, unaccountably, a feeling or urgency to leave came over him - a sense of being a trespasser in this small Eden. He sat quietly for awhile trying to analyze the situation and then rose and walked about scanning the canyon walls. He finally concluded that there was no better way out than the one he had used to get in. So he climbed up and out. He stopped to look down once again and thought he would return another day. He never did this. Perhaps another event of the day had a bearing on this.

Upon returning to his small camp he found his tent a shambles due definitely to a marauding bear. There were tracks about and, in picking up a can that had contained syrup, he found teeth and claw punctures. Bear dote on sweets!

Epilogue

I walked east over the hill to Clear Creek this afternoon - for years a favorite and frequent thing to do - and now I sit atop a rock.

At my feet is a patch of purple asters, autumn's last offering of the floral world; and, in attendance, is a beautiful bronze-and-black butterfly. I regret the change of name - it used to be "flutter-by."

Before me lies the panorama of the ranch. It is a lovely afternoon - blue October sky with a few scattered, fluffy clouds; the air, warm and sweet enough to wrap a baby in. And so very still! So different from the springtime teeming with the business of bird nesting, leafing, cabin cleaning, and calf time. All that is over and done.

The meadow looks smooth as a rug - a soft golden tan - and the haystacks dot it in comforting number. Nothing is more satisfying to us cattle folks than plenty of hay piled up for the winter sure to come. Each stack has its soft gray aspen fence, and inside that one, another of elk panels—just in case! There do not seem to be many elk in our area now, but let an old-time winter of deep snows come, and down come the creatures - thirty, fifty, a hundred! Though hungry, they will eat only choice morsels, picking the haystacks apart and then gamboling over the remains like romping children leaving a mess that is almost impossible to feed to cattle.

The little lake is a mirror, blue as the sky and reflecting its clouds—not a ripple stirring.

A lone bluebird flies by. Is it a parent, its brood reared and gone, haunting the scenes of summer, I wonder? If so, where is its mate? Just over the rise of this little hill, waiting, I hope.

The cabins have that drowsy stillness of vacancy. No smoke curls from their chimneys, no screen doors slam, no voices disturb the quiet, yet a feeling comes to me that if I were to enter their doors I would find the summer occupants there, stored and folded with the blankets. It is not a bad feeling -they are all such wonderful friends!

Even the highway is devoid of traffic, and this is Sunday afternoon! Everyone seems to have gone where he was going yesterday, probably deer and elk hunting on the other side of the pass, where the "season" opened yesterday. I am glad, for the road is free of dust clouds today.

The leaves have gone from the aspen, except in a few places; and yet their going seems not to have detracted from the beauty of the surrounding hills waiting so quietly in the sunshine and shadows. But now I hear sounds: cattle bawling and the voices of men bringing the last of the Clear Creek Pool stock over the ridge north. Yes! There, I see them!

A wind has been stirring the trees along Clear Creek east of me. A truck is coming in from the south pasture - Warren returning from a fence-fixing job.

It is four o'clock, and if the chicken I fry for supper is to have proper cooking, I'd best be going home, west.

GUNNISON HIGH SCHOOL
800 WEST OHIO
GUNNISON, CO 81230

18083145R00081

Made in the USA
Middletown, DE
21 February 2015